GodSpeak

. . .I AM

A Book of Devotions
When God Speaks In Silence

Ron P. Wallace

Burkhart Books

Bedford, TX
www.burkhartbooks.com

*The God of Israel, the Savior, is
sometimes a God that hides Himself,
but never a God that is absent;
sometimes in the dark,
but never at a distance.*

Matthew Henry

Dedications

To my GRANDest children in their birth order
    Pace Vaughn Stollenwerk
    Hayden Dianne Wallace
    Drake Josef Stollenwerk
    Carson Joseph Wallace
    Hudson Bauer Stollenwerk

May you always know how much I love you, and especially the unconditional love of our heavenly Father. My prayer is that He will be with you all the days of your lives and that you will dwell in His presence forever.

Acknowledgements

This book was written at the gentle, but persistent urging of my wife and best friend, Lois Jane Wallace. Her faith continues to stand the test of time, who remains steadfast and faithful to our heavenly Father. Lois Jane is a living testimony of what He desires of His children. Thank you for your love of our Savior and for me..

The dark night of the soul has become all too common during my lifetime. If you have been there, you know. I don't need to say anymore. If you have never experienced it over a long period of time, pray you will never be left alone in silence.

It was during those silent times God sometimes spoke to me the loudest, when there was no one else allowed to be with me. This devotion book includes those words He spoke to me. Although I was alone, God never left me. Neither did Lois Jane. I am very thankful.

A special acknowledgement also goes to Tim Taylor of Burkhart Books. Thank you, Tim, for your friendship and untiring efforts to make this book possible as well as the earlier devotion book, *Encouraging Words In A Discouraging World*. You are a true gentleman and scholar.

Tim and his wife, Michelle, walked through the valley of shadow of death with me. It was during the untimely death of Dianne at the age of 47, my high school sweetheart and first wife. Both of you will always be special to my family.

Foreword

When you've done all you can do to pursue God, what is there left to do? There is nothing else you can say, nowhere to go, and not another turn you can make. You are alone with no more options.

The journey now has you at a dead end. There is not another turn you can make. You stand in total silence, alone before a silent God.

You feel separated from a God you thought you knew. Now you don't know. You don't even know what you thought you knew. And you certainly don't know about this God anymore.

It is during this silence that you can hear the most. His voice may no longer be giving direction or inspiration. But He's still God. He wants to speak now to you, even if it is in a still small voice.

God will meet you on the darkest night in the darkest place of your life. He wants you alone with Him. If this is where He brought you, then this is where you need to be.

GodSpeak shares the intimacy felt during those times of isolation. The dark night of the soul is real, but so is His presence. Read these words while you listen for His voice. God does hear. He does speak. You will sometimes experience His clearest revelation when silence becomes the loudest thing you hear.

Ron P. Wallace

GodSpeak...I AM

January 1

A new year means new beginnings. Things to be experienced in the future will be unlike some of the things in the past. Be mindful of My work in your life and My plans that are about to unfold.

Be mindful of My Word and My words this year. As I write them on your heart, write them down as a remembrance. My Word is the holy Scriptures and My words are those things I speak to your spirit.

Each year brings a new season. In order to bear fruit, you must also bear the pruning knife. I only cut the limbs that are potential fruit bearers.

Your responsibility in life is to bear fruit in My kingdom. Scars in the past will not go unnoticed by Me. Others will now see the harvest as I unfold those things that are of Me and a result of My pruning.

January 2

Doubts are stones that you hurl at other people when you have doubts of your own. Doubts can send you into a storm or cause you to encounter desert dry land. You see no means of being rescued by Me because of the silent doubts you have about My actual existence.

The only thing you may have to go on is My word in My Word. I have spoken through the ages and choose when, where, and how I speak today.

For the moment it may be a matter of survival. I have never abandoned you. Because you are My child, I only ask for simple faith. That's what gets you to heaven and that is what will get you to the other side.

Anyone can doubt, but not all have the faith it takes. I will show you a better way. Don't give up the faith. That's all you have. That's all I need.

January 3

You have sought Me and you can't seem to find Me. I AM not lost and neither are you. You seek Me more earnestly when I become silent and that's what I choose to do from time to time. When you have nothing else left you can say to Me, I can then to speak to you.

I am not a short order God where you throw your requests quickly to me and then hurriedly wait for an immediate response. Waiting may take longer than minutes. It may turn into months and stretch into years. I see your dilemma. I hear your prayers. And yet I may still choose not to respond or change your present circumstances.

You may have no choice but to wait for the moment. Any earlier move causes the process to begin all over again. That causes the wait to be even longer than before.

A promise not fulfilled can result by breaking away from Me. Hold fast to your faith, even if it is smaller than a mustard seed. I can work with that small amount to bring about greater things. Wait and see.

January 4

You look toward the end of your life and don't see a lot. I tell you to look back over your life and see what all I have done for you. I revealed Myself even when you had doubts.

You doubted Me then and you still doubt Me now. You are forgiven for your wayward thinking and way of living. Some of My greatest followers were those with the greatest doubts. Doubts are part of life. So is My forgiveness.

You must not stop now because My plans for you have not been removed. They are still in place and you must continue to move forward for them to come to pass. Live by faith. Also, lead others by speaking your faith.

You can speak things into existence by faith, prayer, and speaking My words given to you. Believe when there is nothing left to believe.

I look for people of faith, even a person of faith. If you believe, then you can do, even when others don't see how anything else can be done.

January 5

Look unto the hills where your strength comes from. The hills are the high places and that is where you are to worship Me. As your worship is offered, so is My strength to you. My blessings also flow from there.

The more you worship, the more you will know Me. That's where I make Myself known. Gather into My presence and offer your praise and worship. That's where I reveal more of Myself to those who truly want to worship Me.

Don't let this day go by without entering into My presence with praise and worship. That's what I desire from you. That's what I wait for.

January 6

I will always be with you although I will not always make My presence known. Not experiencing Me can be like a barren land you are crossing with no means of quenching your spiritual thirst.

You desperately need a drop of My presence. That can only come from Me when I choose.

The less I make Myself known, the more you see the importance of Me in your life. Even small revelations are valued more than ever before. Dryness will cause you to become desperate.

You must walk by faith and not by sight. Be at peace. Be at rest. Give Me now even a drop of faith and I will begin to send showers of blessings.

January 7

Be anxious for nothing, neither in the physical nor material realm. There is the heavenly realm where kingdom work is also being done. You concern yourself with things that are only seen with the natural eye and heard with the natural ear.

I dwell in the heavenlies and that's where I speak My words into being and do My work. It comes into existence even before it comes to you.

I have total control and nothing happens without My knowledge. I know and I do. There's no reason for you to be anxious.

As things unfold in the heavenlies, so shall you see them on earth. I've established My kingdom in the hearts of those who believe in Me. Nothing has ever happened in your life that I was never aware of its existence. And it never will.

Be at peace today although things around you seem to be in chaos and turmoil. This is when My children will know My love and My protection for them. Worry and anxiety change nothing.

Only I will allow those things needed to conform you into the likeness of My Son. Follow His example. Fear not, for I AM with you this very moment.

January 8

I AM the Author and Finisher of your faith. It begins with Me and it ends with Me. Your faith began in Me when you believed in My beloved Son. It begins with Him and must continue with Him, even this very day.

Humanity and the frailty of life cause your faith to ebb and flow. Like the moon and the tide, it is affected by unseen forces. Although your world may seem chaotic, I will bring about justice and reward. Nothing will go unnoticed and everything will be accounted for and brought into judgment.

You don't have control over the events in your life, but you do choose how to respond. Make it a life worth living by living a life of faith in Me. That's where it began and where it must continue.

Your faith must be in Me until the end. That's why I AM to be the finisher of your faith also. Finish the race and finish it with faith in Me.

January 9

You have not been rejected, but selected. You have been chosen because of My own choosing. You are gifted for the task. You are equipped for the endeavors ahead of you. It's not about the giants surrounding you, but Me, who is in you. I AM bigger than any giant or mountain between you and your calling.

Every day is a battle, but it's also an opportunity to see how I work in and through your circumstances. Don't compare yourself. The callings and vocations in life of others are different than yours.

You are not to compare gifts or the calling. They are unique to each individual. My work and My timing in your life is different from others. None of it is the same because no one is exactly the same.

You wonder how much longer. It's less than ever before. Each day is a day closer and brings you closer to Me.

Don't give up. Don't walk away from the prize that is set before you. You are My prized possession and I have so much more I want you to experience.

Make this day one you will believe more and question less. Questions don't always provide answers.

For the moment you don't know all, but at some point it will be made known. That's why you'll be able to see I was there all the time, even from the beginning. Wait and see.

January 10

"Fear not." I've pronounced that to many of My children who experienced fear. Fear is the opposite of faith. I can work with your faith, but the enemy works with your fear.

How can you follow if you don't trust Me? How can you overcome your enemies with fear? That fear can overcome you and bring you down in defeat.

Others watch and see how you outwardly respond to adversity. I see on the inside. I see inside your mind where your thoughts reside. It's in your thoughts where your faith resides. That's where it intersects with My power.

You can overcome any adversity if you believe in Me. Don't let this be a day where the enemy gains ground in your thoughts. Instead, let it be one where you advance My kingdom on earth.

It's through you that the darkness of the enemy can be driven back and My power illuminates the way and exposes the traps of the enemy. Let faith reign in your life that will cause fear to retreat into its own darkness.

January 11

The day will come when you will see what I have been doing all along. My power and strength that lie within you is the same that dwelled with the first disciples and those who were martyred for My name's sake. They did not live faithless lives, but lived for Me.

Take up your cross and follow Me. I will lead you to more truth and better understanding. What you experience is only for a season. Joy will come in the morning. Morning is when My light and My word overcome darkness and the dark side of your life.

Allow what is not of Me to be exposed to My truths. Let Me reveal what needs to be dealt with. Once it has been confessed and forgiveness has covered it, then is when you can go forward in full strength and not have to retreat back in the shadows.

My light not only brings clarity, but also warmth. Allow Me to wrap you in My love and My promises. They can keep the enemy's fiery darts from doing you harm. I AM your Protector for this day and for this time in your life.

Watch your enemies scatter when you remind them of My Word and how they were defeated at Calvary. They will have no power over you if you exercise My power within you.

January 12

You may wonder why I brought you to this point in life. There is a purpose of where you are, but just as important is the path that brought you here.

The destination of a trip is most important, but so is the direction. One way may take you through more valleys, while another encounters straighter paths. It's all part of My plan for your life.

You would not be ready for the lessons and experiences I have for you now if you had not taken the path so designated for you. My path causes you to experience highs and lows to teach you the needed lessons in life.

I have placed an oasis at the point in time to quench your spiritual thirst. I also provided lush valleys before encountering barren land. I know what's needed and where you need to be.

Tomorrow will be another day, but it will also be another step along the way. If you have trusted Me, you are closer than you have ever been. Life has a limited number of days, so make each day count for Me. Even now you will see what I AM doing. Trust Me. I know what I AM doing at this very moment in your life.

January 13

Before you look which way to go, look to Me. I have determined the beginning and the ending points for your life.

What you do in between is what counts. Make the best of every moment and make it count for Me. Forget the past and move forward. You cannot undo what you've done, but I can do something new. Let Me begin today, for I know how it will all end.

January 14

I have prepared a way for you because I AM the Way. I will not lead you astray, for I know the Truth. If you choose this way, I will give you life, because I AM Life.

You have been prepared for such a time as this. No longer doubt your calling or My direction. Be still and know My heart so you can know My will. That defines who you are and what life is to be about for you.

Make today count for Me and all these other things will be added unto you.

January 15

You feel as if life has consisted of mainly a rainstorm. Within the rain are My mercy drops. I have already showered you with My mercy that will allow you to live another day.

It's not what you think you deserve, but what I desire for you. My desire goes beyond what you can ever dream is possible. I have more for you than your mind could ever comprehend.

Allow Me to work outside the capacity of your mind. My thoughts go beyond the universe, so why do you try to contain Me with your finite mind?

Choose this day for Me to show you what I can do. It

may be in a simple, but yet quiet way. You will know it's Me if you listen for My voice and look for Me. I will not disappoint you if you believe in Me to show you the way.

January 16

Doubts about who you are may cause you to doubt who I AM. Do not mistake My identity. And do not underestimate the power I have in your life and the potential you have in Me.

Do not be afraid to ask. Do not have the fear of being disappointed. I AM an unlimited God and there's nothing too big for Me. And neither is there a request too small for Me. You wait on Me, but I AM waiting on you. Trust Me to meet your needs. Believe in Me and pursue Me.

The more you move toward Me, the more I can move you into kingdom work and all the blessings for those who labor for Me. My work does not bring about stress or anxiety.

January 17

My peace for you can be for today. Do not let your heart be troubled. I AM God. I can take care of your troubles. I will not give you a glimpse of My glory if you only depend upon your own understanding.

Let go of your doubts and let Me show you. Nothing comes your way that I don't know about. Believe Me when I say I know what is best for you. But doing so, you will not go the wrong way or make an incorrect decision. But it only comes about in My time.

Trust My decisions, but you must also trust My timing. You will see what I can do and why it is for such a time as this. I will do no more than I need to do, but will bring into being what needs to be done.

January 18

There are some things you want to know, but I have chosen to make some of those things unknown. Some things will cause you to run ahead of Me. Other things may bring about confusion for the moment.

I had to wait for you to reach this point because you were not ready for full disclosure. I will now begin to reveal more of My ways for you to move.

Do not try to bring along others who do not have the same calling. They will not understand My direction because they do not know My voice for this particular calling.

Days of testing will always be in front of you, but some of the toughest testing will soon be behind you. Don't stop at this time, but choose to move ahead again tomorrow.

A mountaintop experience is on the horizon. Move from the shadows in the valley to the shadows of the mountain where you will be able to better see what I was doing all along.

January 19

Rest in My arms. Cover yourself with My protection. No one can remove that purpose I placed in you nor the passion of your desire for Me. That is what pleases Me. Maintain your pursuit and then I will pour blessings upon blessings on you.

You will know My love for you in a dimension you've never known before. You will soon see and know.

January 20

A wrong decision by you while in pursuit of Me does not constitute an end to the purpose that I created you. Repentance brings about restoration. Renew your mind and your efforts to follow Me once again.

Your mistakes may cause for a pause, but it doesn't bring to an end what I have begun in you. The pause is only temporary, so set your face once again toward the overflow on the other side of this juncture.

If you choose not to move on, the brook of blessings beside you will soon run dry like it did for Elijah. Go where I direct you. There a miracle awaits you that will not only bless you, but will benefit others also.

Do not get distracted by people or discouraged by circumstances from what I have deeply imbedded in your spirit. Move on as I move you to others things.

January 21

Be of good cheer, for I have overcome the world. You are an overcomer in My kingdom's work. There are mountains that must be overcome. That's why I give you the command, "Say to the mountain and it shall be removed."

You speak to your mountain today. Don't talk to others about the obstacle you are facing. It can be moved or I would not have given you the command to speak to it.

The mountain is of no importance. What is important is what lies beyond it. That's where the blessings I have for you await.

Not everyone will receive what I have for them, only the ones who speak with authority and in My name. Believe in Me and believe that you can overcome anything in My name.

January 22

I made life a journey that has direction and a destination. You must know the direction to reach the destination. But direction becomes unknown at times.

That's how faith is built. You walk by faith when you don't know where My steps are taking you. I have determined the path you are to travel. My path leads you to do the work of the kingdom while on earth.

If you are not doing My work, then you've taken your own path that will ultimately lead to destruction. Your purpose is to be fulfilled while on earth and not just when you get to heaven. It is now. It is for such a time as this.

Look for Me everywhere and every day. Look all around you as I make My presence known. I AM not only in the good things, but also the things that seemingly go wrong.

Your most recent tragedy can turn into a triumph if you allow Me to use it for My kingdom's work. Walk in the light I've given you, even if it's only enough to take one step. Make that step toward Me today. That will be one more day and one more step closer to better understanding My ways.

January 23

A day of hope is also a day of mercy. The hope you have is a way of giving mercy to you. My mercy allows you to live another day and a reason for that additional day in your life. Without My mercy, there would be no more days in your life.

None of your days are to be wasted, not even today. If you have little hope of life getting better, then you have misplaced hope. Hope should be placed in Me and no one else. Others will disappoint you. You may not understand My workings in your life, but you must trust Me.

I have extended My mercy to you. That's why I have given you another day to your life. Make it count for Me with what you know and where you are.

January 24

Betrayal can take the life out of you. It took the life out of My Son, but it didn't come as a surprise. I used the work of others to bring about My will on earth.

You say you will never forget what was done to you. It's not about forgetting, but about forgiving. My Son asked Me to forgive those who crucified Him. You must follow His example and ask Me to forgive those who tried to take the life out of you.

Your forgiveness of them is also what I wait for from you. The root of bitterness in you may end up being your own poison. Vengeance will be Mine to those who rise up against Me. You will be vindicated for what is done in My name and for My work on earth.

Be cleansed in the waters of My forgiveness and let it flow to your enemies. Wash yourself of that bitterness and hatred to others. Replace it with My forgiveness that freely flows down from My rivers of mercy.

January 25

Living can take the life out of you, but that's not My way for you. I give you life so you can live it abundantly. I will never abandon nor forsake you. Those thoughts are not from Me, but from the enemy who wants you to give up on Me.

I have you in the palm of My hand while My other hand surrounds you and covers you with My protection. No one can touch you without My permission.

If your life doesn't seem worth living, then give it to Me. See what I can do when you live for Me. I breathe the breath of My life into you once again. Allow it to give you new meaning and then live it for Me. Take it from Me and don't allow others to take any more life from you.

January 26

I have called you out from among others, but I also send you back to live with them. A light shines the brightest where it is the darkest. Your life is about directing others to Me and living for Me.

Along the way you'll see people searching for Me. Tell others your story about the way your life has changed and is now about Me. What you experience with Me is more than a thing of the past. It's about the present. It's what I AM doing now for you.

Ask for My will to be done in your life. I will only do as much as you allow. I can do more if you want to experience more of Me. Make that decision and stay fully committed to My calling. That will be a story you can tell wherever you go.

January 27

Following Me is a calling with a cost. No true disciple escapes this world without paying a price. It cost My Son while on this earth as well as My disciples. The same will be true for you.

For some, it has already been a high price. For others, the testing is yet to come. What you experience will either set you apart or let you see how much of the world is still in you.

Be thankful for the tribulations and dark valleys you encounter along the way. That shows you how much aware I AM of you and what you are going through.

It's not by accident that I have chosen this way while on your journey in life. Others seem to have it much easier and their load is lighter. It's because they have chosen not to pay the price, but to focus on the gains this world offers. But it will be burned away.

They will have nothing to show for what they thought they deserved. They do not desire the blood shed by My Son because they thought there was another way to Me.

You measure success by monetary gain. That is merely wood and hay to Me. It can be burned away quicker than it can be accumulated. You say you have needs. I AM the One who can supply more than needs.

But there is more to life than what you can gain. It's about what you can give away in My name. What you choose to do for others, you do for Me. What you can do in My name is what I long to see.

That is what counts in My kingdom and that's what you can present to Me on your day of accounting. It will be in your future, so be prepared.

January 28

Every sparrow that has fallen did so under My watchful eye. I have seen the times you have fallen, but you have not failed. You wonder how you could have made such a downward spiral. It's not about the distance you fell, but the journey back to Me.

Every journey you take has its curves and twists. There will be days where you are in the valley. Even death, at times, may try to overshadow you. But be not discouraged. I not only created life, but even death has been conquered through My loving Son.

Trust Me to show you the way back to Me. I have more for you to live than just today. Tomorrow is another day to live for Me and complete that which I called you to do.

Bring praise to My holy name today, be filled with My Spirit and encounter My presence.

January 29

Not everyone who calls Me, "Lord", will enter into heaven. It is only for those who have a heart for Me and I call, "child."

My children know My name and know they have been called. Their calling has been followed with a commitment only to Me and not the things of this world. It's not an easy call and not all will enter into My gates.

See where your commitment lies and what your values

are in life. You may lose your life for Me, but will gain an eternity with Me. Life is like a vapor and it will soon vanish. See what you have done for Me today that will count for tomorrow.

It's not just about what you have done for Me, but why you did it. That's how you will know if I AM truly the Lord of your life and your eternity.

January 30

The questions you have for Me will soon be answered. It causes concern, but it should not affect your commitment. I know about tomorrow and all about eternity. Do not let your concerns go into tomorrow. Today should be enough of your worries.

Tomorrow brings you a day closer to Me where you will one day experience total joy and the purest of love. That's why life is worth living one more day.

Leave your worries at My feet today. There is no need to take them into tomorrow. They will only cause dread and fear. That's not the way you are to experience life and that's not your burden to carry. That is for Me. My shoulders are big enough to carry any load that weighs you down or becomes a distraction.

Such a heavy load will only cause you to look down. You will miss what I AM doing in your life if the weight of the world is too much for you to look into My face. See Me in what I AM doing this very day.

I will reveal Myself to you, but you must be looking for Me. Even the smallest revelations can bring about some of the greatest truths you will ever know. Look today and see what I can do.

January 31

Your day is not just about you living, but you living in Me. I reveal Myself to others through others. You are a chosen earthen vessel that carries the message of salvation and My Spirit.

I choose to make Myself known through those who make a commitment to follow Me. What truths you are allowing Me to reveal to others is a way I reveal Myself.

Don't be afraid to speak My truths. Your commitment is to Me and your loyalty is to be everlasting. I committed Myself to you for an eternity. You cannot lose your way if you follow Me in truth and in spirit. Be sure of your steps and be certain of your commitment this very day.

February 1

You may question your purpose at times, but My presence should never be questioned. As the Creator, I brought you into being. As your Maker, I can make your life into one that can bring glory and be pleasing to Me.

Resting in My presence can bring about more revelation. As I reveal more of Myself to you, the more of My purpose for you in life will be revealed.

Watch Me when I cause My enemies to fall. You have nothing to fear as long as you walk alongside of Me. Live today in My peace and My presence. Experience the life I have for you today, regardless of the time you have left on earth.

February 2

The pain you felt in the past is from the plowing I have done in your life. As the plow moves below the surface, there is an exposure of things that needs to be removed from daily living.

The soil of your mind must be free from the entanglements of life and the things that have become hardened in your life. Situations and relationships sometime turn into stone and hinder My work in your life.

The deeper I plow, the more you will see what is below the surface of your life and the subconscious mind. It must be removed in order for the seed of blessing to be planted.

An entangled and a hardened life yield no harvest. The plowing season will last only as long as it takes to prepare for the planting. A blessing will come today from where I plowed yesterday. The produce will far exceed the pain. Share your yield with someone today who feels they are being plowed under. You will both be blessed.

February 3

Looking back is not for you to see what you haven't done. Instead, it's for you to see where you have been. Looking ahead is not for you to see what needs to be done, but where I AM sending you.

The task can be overwhelming, but each day brings another revelation of what your life is about and what I have called you to do. Past assignments are now in the past. You cannot live tomorrow over again.

Looking back will also not allow you to see what is ahead. The most beautiful sunrises are yet to be seen. The most fulfilling days are still to be lived.

Only look back to see My mercy and Me guiding you through those storms. See the good things I have done. Now look for the better things that lie ahead, things that will bring about a closer walk and a nearness of My presence.

February 4

Your joy is not to be dependent on others. Happiness in

life is not about them, but about Me. Trying to please everyone will only bring about disappointment.

Your eyes on Me keep you from looking to others. The direction I have for you is not dictated by them. They may lead you into a ditch or cause you to get stuck in a rut. How can others help you when they can't even see their dilemma?

You have shoes of the gospel so you can share the Good News. Don't look at today as a day of getting from Me. Use it to give My love to those who don't know it. The more you give to them, the more I can give to you. Experience the overflow I have for you as My love flows through you to others.

February 5

I AM the Light of the world and My light shines through you. Don't look for light in the world, but be My light while in the world. As the world becomes darker, you are to penetrate that darkness.

Turn your heart toward Me and I will direct your steps. The path may be narrow and even crooked, but it will lead straight to me. Keep your footing on the solid rock of My Word. It will keep you from sinking into the non-essentials of everyday living.

Place your trust in Me and don't allow the enemy to put doubt in your mind. A wavering mind will cause you to stumble. A wandering spirit will lead to a downfall. Be sure of your relationship to Me and be solid in your commitment. Your safety and your security lie in Me.

February 6

Failure comes when you fail to realize I AM the Author of your life. I designed your characteristics and I diagrammed your journey. You are no accident, but you are a part of My plan.

I never ask the question, "Why?" about you because I know who you are and whose you are. You are Mine and My creation. Each of My creations starts in My mind.

Live for Me so My love can be seen through you. Show them the way to Me is through My Son, Jesus. Direct others to Me when I send you to them.

Your path will cross with others who are at an intersection in life. Show them the way by telling them of My love. No one has wandered too far or sunk so low that they can't be redeemed and restored by Me.

February 7

People look around on the outside world to find answers to life. The answer lies on the inside. My Spirit has never left you, so there is no reason to look anywhere.

Look on the inside. It is there to guide your mind and your thoughts. Your help comes from within, because there is where I dwell. I will be your guide, for I AM the Way. I will lead you to the answers of your questions because I AM the Truth.

Outside of Me, only death exists, because I AM the Life. I will always have your interest at heart because you are My cherished creation. Nothing will ever be able to release you from My grasp. I hold you as the most precious thing in My possession.

Others can only speculate about My relationship to you. No one has been able to see inside of Me in order to see how I love and care for you. No one can do anymore than I've done for you. And no one can love you more than I love you.

February 8

You have called Me by name, and I call you by name, a follower. You chose to follow Me when you called upon Me.

But I called you first.

A follower must trust the One that you follow. You must trust Me to lead you on the path that I ordained for you. I knew this is where you would be before I created you. You are here where you are, calling on My name. This is why you call Me, because I have called you for a purpose for such a time as this.

Not only listen, but look where I AM directing you. It's here at this place in your life that you will better understand what I have been doing all along. Trust Me for the work that I now entrust you to do for Me.

February 9

I created you in a way that will bring about My kingdom's work on earth. Everyone who is a follower of Me has a specific calling and purpose for such a time as this.

My plans are carried out by My people. What I want to bring about at this time in My creation includes you. No one is too small for a task. No one is to think of themselves as too big or too significant for an assignment. Such thinking can disqualify them from Me doing a future work.

It was pride that brought about the downfall of Lucifer. It originated in his thinking. Let My thoughts be your thoughts. A prideful thought brings about rebellion, and rebellion will not allow you to be a part of My kingdom. Align whatever you say or do with My Word and My words. That will keep you from rebellion that will lead to a fall.

February 10

Your work on earth is not done. There is more to do and that is the reason I have given you another day. Don't look beyond today for your future. Your future is today, this very moment.

What you experienced in the past is why you are here today. I've taught you things that can be an example to others. Your life is your testimony. That is what speaks to others. What is it saying to others? What does it say about Me?

While some may not read My Word, they are reading your life. It says volumes about your life in relation to Me. Let them sense My peace within you and not confusion that only comes from the enemy.

I hold you in My hand and no one can remove you. No one can remove My peace from you without your permission. I've given My peace to you, so now take it and wrap it around you. You can experience it more than ever before. Go now in peace.

February 11

Darkness has a way of entering the mind, just as it entered the world. It enters through your thinking. That is why you are to guard your mind from thoughts that are not My thoughts.

Darkness may overcome areas of light, but it will never completely cover the light. There will always be light somewhere in the world.

The enemy will try to come over you, but he will never fully overcome because I have overcome the world and darkness.

A light shines the brightest wherever it is the darkest. Although the enemy may have darkened your path, I will always be there to guide you through those dark moments. Walk in the light that I have given you and it will take you to more light that will soon give clearer direction.

February 12

My Son told you not to be troubled. He was not only the Way, but He showed the way. He is the only way to heaven and to Me. Why would you believe anyone else who is not from Me? He experienced death for you so you could have life in Me and with Me.

Don't consider yourself a victim, but one who has victory. Death has been overcome, so your life doesn't end on earth. Although life may not have a lot of meaning for the moment, you will soon see the real meaning of life. Look to no one and nothing else. Look only to Me.

Others can only promise false hope. Place your hope in Me. Real hope comes from Me because I know what you can experience. Renew your hope in Me because I can give you new life with real meaning. Anything outside of Me is meaningless.

February 13

Life is not about how long you live, but how you live it for Me. I can make more out of your life because I created you. Behind every created being is a reason for being. I have plans for you still to be fulfilled. You may have missed some of them along the way, but you haven't missed Me.

I AM with you every step on the way. You must be aware of My presence and know that I AM working in you and all along the way.

Don't be deceived. Whatever is real from Me will sometimes be counterfeited as a deception from the enemy of this world. You must distinguish what is Me. You can only do this if you are sensitive to the voice of My Spirit within you. I will never deceive you. Neither will I harm you.

Your adversary seeks to destroy you and your testimony. Nothing good will come from him, only lies and deception.

He laughs when he deceives you and causes you to believe a lie. Nothing he says will ever be true. Never believe him and you will never believe any of his lies.

February 14

Why do you believe in Me, yet not believe all the things I can do? No miracle is more difficult than another. I spoke the oceans into existence and spoke the mountains into place. It took no effort on My part.

The most difficult undertaking you could ever ask from Me is the most simple. But I tell you to have a simple faith. Simple faith is simply believing in Me. You know I can do all things and there is much more I can bring about in your life.

Choose this day to believe and make known your faith. Let others see it, and then see what I can do for you. Speak with faith and I will speak to your needs.

February 15

I AM the Creator of the universe and I created you. Along with your creation comes a calling. To fulfill a calling, there must be a commitment. Your commitment is to continue for as long as you live.

Some commit themselves earlier to Me in life. They are able to see much of My kingdom on earth. It lives within them and that's where I choose for My work on earth to be done.

Others give up on their commitments before their lives come to an end on earth. Don't let your commitment end before your life ends. Much of what I want to do is sometimes saved for the later years of life.

If your commitment doesn't last that long, then those special blessings will never come to you. That's why many are disappointed in the way their lives end. It's because their commitments didn't last until the end.

The battle does become weary. The sword may seem too heavy to swing another time. My strength can become your strength. You can do all things through Me, but you must be committed to do what is left to be done.

February 16

Listen for My voice. If you know Me, you know My voice. It is heard in different ways because I speak the way you best hear from Me. Whatever way I choose to speak, you must be willing to wait for Me.

Relationships take time to develop. Take the time to know Me. The more you know Me, the more you can hear from Me. An intimate relationship is not developed by rushing into My presence to make your needs known. You need to know My heart. That's how you can know Me.

Express your love for Me. Enter into My presence with a thankful heart and your voice full of praise. I want time with you more than you want your greatest need to be fulfilled.

Speak to Me now the things I desire to hear from you. Make your praises known to Me and I will make more of Myself known to you. Open up your heart and let your worship of Me flow. Then I will open the doors of heaven from where all blessings flow.

February 17

You've seen the prayers of other believers answered. You question Me and the encounters others have with Me. In your mind you think about some of these as just being a coincidence because you've not seen some of your prayers answered. Such thinking can have severe consequences.

You will miss out on more than what you have already

been given. I dispense the blessings, but there must also be a release of your faith. Unbelief does not set good things from Me in motion. It only serves as an obstacle.

More could be given if you give Me more of your faith. My Son kept bringing into question the unbelief of His disciples. He was present, but their faith sometimes was missing.

Faith can be strong enough to walk on water. Yet it can be simple enough to believe for daily bread. Believe for more today than you believed yesterday. My supply is limitless, so don't be limited by your faith.

February 18

Your anointing sets you apart from your brothers and sisters in Christ, just like it separated David from his brothers. I knew all of David's failures before He would ever experience them. Everyone has failures, but not all has faith.

David had a heart after Me. That's what separated him and that's why I chose to set him apart. A kingdom came forth and was set apart.

David was anointed with oil and the anointing came upon him. My Spirit came upon him and the course of history was changed.

I can change your life if you choose to let Me come upon all of you. The oil was poured over the head of David. Let My Spirit cover your mind and way of thinking.

That's how My chosen vessels are set apart. As David made a difference in the world, I can also cause you to make a difference in the world around you.

Bow before Me in total submission. Experience My anointing and see what I can do in the world of possibilities. All things within My will are possible. Only believe.

February 19

Valleys are the lowest points on earth, just as they are in life. Very little sun reaches the lowest levels. The loneliest of times are felt with almost no hope of survival.

You fall on the valley floor with your face to the ground. My presence is not felt and I seem to be nowhere around.

I AM there with you. I not only made the mountains, but also the valleys. Valleys can draw you closer to Me because there are less people. Very few you know are experiencing such a time as this.

I will walk you through this present valley. Life doesn't stop here and this is not where life ends. Through the valley means making it to the other side.

Lift yourself off the valley floor and look for Me. You will sense My presence and see Me with your spirit. I may choose not to speak for the moment, but I will see you through. Take My hand now and I will lead you on.

February 20

My children experienced a time of spiritual dryness while in the desert. My presence was made known as I met their daily needs. It's during these times that you believe I abandoned you.

Today I will give you daily bread. Believe for the spiritual things as well as for the physical things. I will provide the provisions, but you must see the need for My presence. Don't just look for food, but also look for Me.

Spiritual needs are on a daily basis also. Those needs are met when you spend time alone with Me. I AM your source because I AM in Spirit. Don't overlook the spiritual needs by focusing on your physical needs.

Don't worry about tomorrow. It will have enough worries of its own. Don't worry about your needs for today. Ask for your daily bread and believe all things are possible, even those things beyond your daily bread.

February 21

Praise Me at all times and in all things. Voice it to Me when you think there is no reason for praise. Let your worship for Me be heard in the good times and the bad.

I don't bless you just when you're good. They come from Me, even when you're at your worst. The beat of your heart is My blessing to you.

Don't wait for things to get better before you sing praises to My name. That's how you can make it through the tough times.

Giving thanks should never cease. You are never out of My sight and I know all that you experience. I know when you mean it as well as knowing when it's hard to mean it.

Give Me your thanks when there seems to be none to give. I will take what you give Me and will speak blessings upon you even more.

February 22

From the days of your youth, I have watched you. You are endowed with giftings from Me to help bring about My kingdom work. You are My child and also My light that shines in the darkness that others live in all around you.

Use what I have given you to be used this very day. Be a living testimony for Me as long as I give you life. Look for ways to express My love to those around you. It may be in a very simple and short way, but I can use that moment to help another one of My children who is looking for some demonstration of Me to them.

Someone earlier took the time to tell you about Me. Be that someone today for Me. Share something about Me that can gain entrance into a new way of living and a way to know more about Me.

February 23

The uncertainty of Me working in your life causes an uncertainty of how you look at life. You are not in the last phase of your life. Your last breath will take you to a new phase and dimension for you. That is heaven.

Prepare for the new life you will have in Me when you enter into a new relationship where you will experience joy and peace your mind can't comprehend.

Finiteness has limitations. That's why you'll never be able to comprehend what heaven is all about when you try to imagine it down here.

All the suffering you will ever experience will be on earth. I prepared a place so you won't have to suffer endlessly. Pain does bring an awareness of Me. But it also reminds you what a world of sin is like.

My Son experienced the ultimate suffering, more than anyone else will ever know. Through His suffering I made a way for you to one day enter into My kingdom.

Be sure of your salvation. Be aware of wrong doing on earth, but be assured you have a place that awaits you in the heavens.

February 24

Confusion sets in when there is a lack of trust about Me. I know not only you, but your ways. I allow difficulties to arise to show you the trust you don't have in Me. It is nothing I didn't already know, but it is something in you that needs to be identified.

Trusting Me becomes even more important when you see no where to go or no one who can help you. When you launched out into the deep, you had a trust that you knew I was directing you.

The darker and deeper the environment you find yourself in is no time to let your trust in Me to lessen. Even though you feel you have lost your way, I have not lost you. You are still under My watchful eye with My hand protecting you from the unknown.

Don't think about what you have done wrong to get you here. Think what I can do to bring you to the right place, the place I want you to be. Dwelling on the past will only keep you in the past.

I AM no longer on the shore, so there's no need to go back where I AM not to be found. You will find more of Me in the places where fewer people choose to go. I will reveal more of My presence and My power when you take the risk and move out more into the unknown.

I desire to have you in My presence because I have much more blessings that are for the ones who are willing to risk all for Me.

February 25

The forces of evil set a trap for you. They want to show you that I can't depend on you. But I allow it to capture you at times so you will see the need to depend upon Me. What was meant for harm can be used to bring about good.

Be very much aware of My presence. I AM there to direct your mind and your steps. If you become a victim to the schemes of the devil, I can set you free and make you spiritually stronger. Adversity can be a sharpening tool to make you a force that can bring about more of My kingdom on earth.

Stay no longer in the pit of guilt and humiliation. The longer you stay, the more you see yourself as a victim of your circumstances. Become a victor and not a victim.

See all the good I have done in your life and not on what you think you've done bad. Good can come out of this situation, regardless of your current circumstances. Move your thoughts away from things that cloud your mind.

Let the light of My love drive away the sad thoughts and the clouds of darkness hovering over your mind. Renew your mind and I will renew your reason for being. I can make all things work for My benefit and for your spiritual maturity.

February 26

I have set you aside for such a time. I made you to take part in My purpose that is unfolding before you this very day. You had so many questions leading up to this time. I chose to remain silent at times, leaving you to wonder about My existence and our relationship.

I wanted perseverance to be a part of you. You had to experience it yourself to see that you can make it through difficult times and through those days of hearing nothing from Me.

Let your strength come from not giving up during the times when others have fallen away. Go forth with My Word in your hand and My Spirit as your armor. Fight the good fight and know that in Me you have victory in the coming days ahead.

February 27

Don't have doubts about My existence, My Son, and My purpose for your life. Because your ways are not My ways, the way I AM leading you does not always seem the right direction. Your life does have a specific end as well as a purposed means for the direction I lead you.

Along the way, you have to develop more trust. Your lack of trust only delays what I have for you. Do not be tossed by the winds of emotions and feelings. That can cause ultimate shipwreck. I can calm the fiercest storm with a spoken word into your world. Know that all things are under My control.

Let others sense a peace about you because of My peace that is within you. You may never fully understand the specific storms, but they were placed at specific times and specific locations to bring you into the harbor of safety and love. It's the place where you will know peace and ultimately My purpose.

Be at peace now, for I AM with you to the very end.

February 28

My children experienced My blessings while in the wilderness. You don't have to wait until you reach the Promised Land to receive My provisions and blessings. Look around you and see where I have given things that you never saw as coming from Me.

The clothes you wore today and the food you ate are part of My blessings. A covering for your head was provided along the way.

Don't neglect in recognizing what you consider as a given. I gave it to you for this day. Instead of looking forward to find more, look up today and share your thanks for what you have this very moment.

I AM a God of Blessings. My blessings are bountiful and the supply is endless. Be thankful for this very moment of life and for this day's bread. Tomorrow is another day. It will take care of itself.

March 1

I AM the Vine. Your life comes from Me. Life begins with Me and it ends with Me. I AM the Sustainer that provides life to you, even today.

Life is precious and you are a created being. The life you have today is from Me. You don't have to work at living. It's not something you can create or bring about. You can't even lengthen your life beyond today. It is a gift from Me.

To sustain your life and yourself, you must abide in Me. You rest in Me. You draw strength and substance from Me. I AM your only true source. Everything outside of Me will result in confusion.

March 2

The best for your life is still yet to come. It doesn't matter about your age, your situation, the storms, or the sins you have seriously grieved over. It is measured by the relationship you have established with Me.

Focusing on success and wealth is not the standard I use. I look on the inside at your heart. That's why I can see how you are currently viewing your life.

You have touched some lives, but you can touch more, many more. Take the passion for living and place it into something that will make Me known to others.

Recognize what I've done for you. Tell others, not only about your blessings, but the Source of your blessings.

Humility is a doorway which allows Me to enter into your world. Pride will cause Me to exit quickly where you will have to deal with the aftermath alone.

Purpose in your heart to live for Me. I will prepare the way once again for you to pursue. Don't be dismayed, but see this very day what I reveal as part of My plan.

March 3

You search for Me with your prayers. You look for Me in the heavens. I made Myself known to you and I hear your prayers and see your searching heart. At times, you wonder if I hear you. When you have doubts about My existence, that means there is no one to hear your prayers or rescue you from present troubles.

My existence does not depend on what you believe. But sometimes your prayers are answered by how you believe. Believe in Me with your whole heart, even if that is very little for the moment. This time of uncertainly will bring about certain things in your life.

Faith is about the unseen. You don't see much happening, but that does not mean I AM not engaged in your life. This time of waiting and uncertainly has a reason. The greater the need can mean an even greater miracle.

Do not be troubled. Believe in Me this very day. For the moment, just know that I AM bringing about a good work that will be coming to you. Your part is just to believe. Do your part and I will do the rest.

March 4

You look around and see things out of control. You wonder where life is going and where it is taking you. It's not about just the direction of the world. It's about your direction.

Things don't happen by chance to My children. Everything is under My control. It's during these difficult circumstances that you make choices. You choose to trust Me or believe in the randomness of life and living.

The darkest hour and your weakest moments may come when you should be having more confirmation than ever before. You've questioned others, "Why don't you believe?" For you, it has turned into personal questions about yourself. "Why can't I believe?" You try, but there's hardly a thread of hope left.

Child, this doesn't diminish My purpose for you and neither My belief in you. I knew this is where you would be and the timing of it.

This is not the time to let go of hope. But it's the time to let go of everything but Me. It's easier to move one along if there's less baggage. Your faith may be drained, but your future still lies ahead with its promises.

You may have forgotten how difficult things have been in the past since they are over and you made it through. It took no effort on My part and neither will it take any concerning the difficult task or lack of faith you now face.

I speak into your world. Watch and see how My faithfulness to you has never faltered nor My purpose for you diminished. You're still on track and I AM always on time.

March 5

What you don't believe now about Me may cause you to doubt who I really was in the past. You question secretly if that was really Me or just the way things turned out. Your questions now cause you to question the past.

I WAS. I AM. I SHALL BE. That has never changed, nor will it ever change. I AM the same even though you may have changed.

Whatever you experience or think doesn't change anything about Me. It only changes the way you feel about Me or how you approach Me. Don't let your questions today cloud the way you see Me tomorrow. I have not changed.

It goes back to experiencing the faith of a little child. A child is precious in My sight. You are that child. I will never make you totally vulnerable to the enemy at any time. That will only bring about death and destruction. Nothing happens without My permission and no one can remove My ultimate protection from you.

Rest in who I AM. Believe what I can do. Trust Me in everything. Do not turn away from Me. Job said, "Though he slay me..." Will you still trust Me like Job? By doing so, you will have much more because I AM a much more God.

March 6

You read in My Word, "Where two or three are gathered…" You may be the only one that knows what you are experiencing. No one knows your thoughts and fears of the future because you cannot share it for fear of rejection or retribution.

I know when no one else knows. I see what can't be seen, and I understand when others have misunderstood you. I already knew, but I want you to make it known to Me.

When we gather in spirit, speak to Me in spirit and in truth. Speak things you've never spoken to anyone. Today is not the first time it will be made known to Me. I've known all along. I wait for you when we gather together in spirit.

A way has already been made. A past promise is about to come to pass. I know how to answer your prayers because I have always known how I would respond.

Don't be surprised how I answer your prayers and how I will make Myself known to you in time. If you already know how I plan to respond, that would only be knowledge.

Step outside your comfort zone and stretch your faith. If your faith fails you, I will lift you up, just as I lifted Peter from the overwhelming waves. Others were there in the boat, but I was the only one that could help them.

I may be the only One that has gathered with you and that's what matters. I will not let you drown. Neither will I let you down once you see what I AM doing all around you.

March 7

It doesn't matter who is against you as long as you know I AM for you. I may not be for all that you do, but I do know what I can do for you. You can't undo what was done in the past because that is history. But I AM the God of your future.

Obstacles can be removed and relationships can be restored by a spoken word from Me. I can change that which was considered permanent. I cannot be outdone or overcome.

Take time to get to know Me. Experience the fullness of life that I can give you the remaining days of your life. It doesn't matter who is your enemy or what comes against you.

You have yet to see the power explosion that can come to you through Me. I can defy the law of gravity and nature. My Son defied death, so no law of man or nature can restrict Me.

Only your faith restricts Me. I choose to let you limit Me, but that doesn't have to be your choice. Choose to believe what I can do for you, regardless of what is against you.

Your choices must align with My kingdom's work on earth. Selfish choices only bring about more self-centered-ness. I will bring about more in your life if your life is more about Me.

March 8

The faith of others in Me may diminish because they don't see what difference I AM making in your life. You tell them you believe Me, but that causes them to believe less in you. It sometimes causes you to believe less in Me.

That doesn't diminish My love for you. I know when you are trying while being tried. I hear your silent cries and see your private shedding of tears. Others can see the hurt on your face, but can't feel the hurt in your heart.

Trying times can either tenderize or toughen your heart toward Me. Some have become so toughened that they don't look for Me or listen to Me anymore. Their changed hearts have changed their outlook on life. To them, it's more about being lucky than being My child.

You're not only unsure about the direction, but you're not even sure about your destination. This is when you must walk by faith, My child. My Word is not a book of folklore, but about those who experienced tougher times, whose hearts remained tender and submissive.

Just as I opened the Red Sea for millions, I can also open a way for you to journey in your pursuit of Me. Even if you feel like you've lost your way, I haven't lost you. And I AM too big to lose. Keep looking for Me all around you.

Listen for My voice as I speak into your spirit and mind. What you will soon see will then allow you to see what I was doing all along. Don't let your faith diminish.

March 9

The struggle between belief and unbelief can cause you to waver. My Word tells of a man who said, "I believe; help my unbelief." You believed some things in the past that you knew could only be Me. But that same belief turned into unbelief about some present things. You don't see anything happening in the natural.

You forget I also operate in the supernatural. Those are things you cannot see, but you can still affect. Unbelief can restrict what I want to bring about. What I can bring about swings on the hinge of faith. Even a little faith can go a long way.

The dimensions of your faith are sometimes miniscule. It's very little. I will work with faith the size of a mustard seed. But I AM the Master Gardener. I've planted much more because I AM a much more God. That's what I look for to grow so you can have much more.

It's not about much more possessions, but much more of My peace. More things don't bring more of My peace. More things don't bring more contentment. More of Me is how you become content, regardless of your circumstances.

Ask for more of Me and I will gladly give more. It also comes about by giving more of yourself to Me. Give Me your worries. Give Me your desires.

Store up treasures for heaven and I will open My storehouse on earth. It never becomes empty because I have so much more. Be content for the moment, but be anticipating much more.

March 10

Doubts can erase the reminders of who I AM and what I have done for you. They will also be a reason why more blessings and more revelations from Me may no longer be recognized.

You are here today and made it to this point because of My grace. The enemy has one focus, and that is to destroy anything of My kingdom and anyone associated with it. The one who is against you is the author of confusion and despair. If he can blind you, then he will also bind you.

Unwrap your mind from those thoughts that are not from Me. It not only binds your thinking, but also your freedom to move forward in My name. My kingdom's work will move forward.

You must not be left in a state of doubt. Any doubt of who I AM will become an entry point for the enemy. He looks for the smallest opening where he can plant a tare in the wheat field of your blessings.

You can't encompass in your mind all that I AM and plan for you to be. I know where you are now and where you can be in the months ahead. You must live daily to reach the place and purpose I have for you. Step today in the light I give you. Darkness cannot hurt you nor penetrate you if you allow Me to be your light for this day.

Search for Me in every circumstance and whatever condition you may be in for the moment. That's where I AM and that is how I work. Look for Me. Recognize Me. Let your faith be restored. Allow all your hope to rest in Me. I AM all you have. That is all you need.

March 11

Nothing can take the place of Me. No one can give you what I have for you and where I can take you on this journey in life. I not only know your destiny in life, but how you are to travel. Conditions and companions may change along the way, but I will remain constant.

You look for consistency and want to be sure I AM who I said I AM and be to you all that you want Me to be. Doubt is the thread that can unravel all that you earlier believed. Why let this doubt destroy all you have come to believe?

The heroes of faith doubted. They doubted themselves and even Me. But they chose to believe when they felt they had no reason to believe any more.

If you choose to believe again this day in My glory and in My power, then nothing can stop you from moving forward once again. I AM all that you have and I AM all that you need.

I will restore once again what has been stolen from you by the enemy. I laugh at what the enemy thought he could do to you without My knowledge. But I will turn My laughter to wrath and cause your enemies to scatter.

I lift you up once again and place your feet on solid ground where your faith shall be restored.

March 12

The way to please Me is to live your life in a way that is pleasing to Me. It doesn't matter how others think you should live. It only matters what I think.

Don't be concerned about how those who know you will view you. They can't see all that I see and all that you can be. Others don't want you to rise above them. That's why they try to keep you below them. It makes them feel higher and above you.

Follow the calling that I have placed in your spirit. That is from Me and can never be taken from you. Don't listen to those who doubt your calling. Many of them don't know their place in life, even though they think you're the one that is out of place.

Show contentment for where you are today and don't be concerned about tomorrow. The following day has enough worries of its own. That can wait for another day.

Make a difference in the world by making a difference for Me. What you know within you can change the world around you when you make a difference with your life.

No one knows better than Me, so listen to no one else but Me. There are things I will tell you that I tell no one else. That's why others don't understand what I AM doing in your life. If you want to make a difference today, then allow Me to continue that good work I began in you earlier.

March 13

You are not alone with your thoughts. I created your mind and I know what you think and how it affects you. Thoughts sometime may take you in a downward spiral.

But I AM there to lift you out of the pit. The darkest days are sometimes those when you are imprisoned mentally while in a pit.

I can rescue you from being confined by your thoughts by just a thought on My part. I don't even have to speak, only think. That's how My thoughts can become your thoughts. You are never alone with what encompasses your mind.

I can break those shackles of self doubt and the chains of confusion. The enemy places those around you, but can never lock them. That comes about when you have more doubt than faith. What doubt has locked can be removed when you remove all doubt about who I AM and what I can do.

March 14

I AM God of the universe and I AM to be the God of your universe. Like the universe, I created you. Your life is a result of Me breathing into your universe.

At times you feel as if life has left you and you don't have a life as you did in the past. You sensed My presence and wanted your life to be all about Me. That's the way it should be lived today. You need Me more than ever before.

I AM still the great I AM, and that will never change, not even if you change the way you see Me. It takes faith to believe, especially when you feel you have nothing to believe in.

I revealed Myself even when My people believed the least. They felt they had no reason to live or go forward anymore in life. That's when I made Myself known once again.

Every day is a holy day in My presence. I AM not limited by a calendar or ways you choose to come before Me on those days. I draw people unto Me. This day I will make more of Myself known if you look for Me.

It will be a way that seems simple. I look for the faith of a child in you. Simple faith is simply believing. Don't complicate it by making faith complex.

March 15

You cannot endure this race of life on your strength alone. It will cause you to falter toward the end. You were never meant to run it alone. My strength will help you make it to the finish line. But you must abide in Me for My strength to be in you.

Your own strength is not self sustaining. It only allows you to get started. That's why so many believers drop out of the race. You can't drop out of life. How you finish is what I AM watching. I AM there to help you.

Draw your strength from Me. It's only a matter of asking

and believing. When you are grafted into Me, I will flow into you. There is no work on your part. When you sleep at night, ask for My Spirit to flow into your spirit, soul, and body. Be filled so you can have a full life.

You can experience internal damage if there is nothing in you to draw from. My Spirit is the oil that flows throughout. My Son's continuous command is, "Be filled with the Holy Spirit." The Spirit is personal and desires to be continuously imparted into you.

You may forget what it is like to have not experienced Me for a long time. It's something you don't want to be without. My Son left His peace on earth. It's there. It has never left. Let it be a part of your thinking. As I dwell within you, let My peace be with you and in you as well.

March 16

A promise from Me is My word that comes true. I have kept My promises because I AM as good as My word.

There are times you feel I have not been faithful to you as promised. You don't see Me nor do you sense Me when you feel like you need Me the most.

Keeping My word doesn't mean I keep you from adversity. The fiery trials are a purifying process every believer must encounter. No one is exempt. Each one is different and yet specific for that time in one's life.

When you look for Me, look back to My promises. They were made to give you hope and should be reflected upon, especially when you sense little or no hope.

Each promise will bring about a God encounter when fulfilled. You will know I kept My word and will cause you to know Me even more. You will realize I didn't forget you. Neither did I forget My promises to you.

I kept My word and will continually keep it. I also kept you while on this journey in life and will continue to the end.

Look ahead and see what I have for you. Also, go back to the promises made earlier to remember what I reminded you of back then.

March 17

Life will sometimes seem to fall apart while pursuing Me. Just when you think you received a revelation, nothing happened. Each day is a daily walk with Me. You can't go on yesterday's experience and you don't know what tomorrow holds.

Today is the day you trust Me for today's daily bread. Yesterday's revelation is stale. It was for that day. I may choose to reveal Myself in a different way. You must look for Me in a way you have never seen before.

Daily dependence is the way you are to live. I know what you need, even before you tell Me. I know what you will experience even before you arrive. That is how I know what you need each day and why it is to be a daily walk.

My Son taught His followers to ask daily for their bread. As you ask, it shall be given to you also. But when you ask, believe in Me and what I can do. Nothing is impossible for Me.

March 18

You made mistakes in the past, even when you thought it was My will. I know each time you made those decisions. I know what was in your heart also. No decision can overshadow Me where I AM unable to respond and restore.

You trusted Me to make the right decision although it now seems very wrong. I can make the worst turn out for the best.

Spend no more time in remorse. Put your trust in Me to turn what you thought was a mistake into something that can work for good. You will see how it will move you to a place I have for you.

Right choices are not the only things that move you ahead. I can use what you considered a wrong choice to put you in the right place and the right position. Wandering should not always cause you to wonder what I AM doing. I AM moving you to the place and purpose I've established for you, even before the beginning of your life.

The hairs of your head are numbered. The days ahead are numbered. You won't come up short if you follow Me. I will have you at the right place. I know where that is. I will also have you there at the right time. I know when that is. Both will soon come to pass, but they must happen at the same time.

March 19

My children call Me by name. They know Me and they know My voice when they hear it. You know it because you've heard it. But the less you hear My voice, the harder it will be to recognize.

You must be in communion with Me each day. Speak to Me, and I will speak to you. Whatever you desire, you must ask. You must also listen for what I desire from you. My desires are much better for you, but you listen less than you speak.

You must listen more today than you did yesterday. You must never cease praying, but you must never stop listening. My Spirit is in you. That's how close I AM to you. That's how near My plans are for you. They are not hidden away from you, but have been placed within you.

March 20

Total dependence is what you strive for, but it's more of a

struggle. You say you depend upon Me when all of life seems to be working in your favor. Real dependency is more than just talk. It's a time of testing.

That's the time when your weaknesses are revealed. It's when you see who you really are and what still needs to be developed or torn down. Sometimes I have to tear down before I can build up.

An unsure foundation will surely bring about a collapse of what was built on it. Test your foundation each day. Look for impure motives and hidden agendas. Search for any cracks or fractures unseen to others.

I will reveal what is exposed to the enemy. It's an area where the enemy is making an inroad. It will bring about a collapse if it is not corrected. Remove it by living holy with a pure heart. A pure heart is more precious to Me than what you try to accomplish for Me.

Let Me show you what you need to know. You must be open and not continue to ignore the warning signs you've noticed along the way. It's for your good. Follow Me with total dependence and I will make good on My word.

You are not to depend upon anyone else's faith. Your faith is to be fully used for such a time as this. I will come through and see that you will make it through.

March 21

People measure your life by your accomplishments. I measure it by your struggles, not just the ones others see, but those that are unknown to anyone else. You know the fears and struggles you face alone. Either no one else is there or no one else knows what you face even now.

You were not made to make it alone. I AM here right now with you as your mind struggles with uncertainty, even a sense of doom. Nothing is too dark or too dangerous if you put all your trust in Me. It's not partial trust, but fully trusting in what I will bring about in your life today.

It must be a total dependence you have in Me, even if you think you need to remove yourself from what I AM allowing you to go through. Don't let fear overcome you. Put your faith once more in Me. I AM all that you have, but I AM all that you need.

March 22

"And lo, I am with you." There are lowly times and lowly places in your life when you don't believe what you used to believe. Nothing makes sense anymore. I AM not confused about what is happening to you. The way that is not clear and the circumstances that don't make any sense don't mean you have lost your way.

The shadows are very long on the valley floor. You look above and you are overshadowed. You know the sun is shining somewhere, but not in your world. You don't need to see the sun to experience Me. I AM with you in your present valley.

Don't look for the sunshine, but listen for Me in the silence of the moment. That's when I may speak quietly, but it is also when you can hear Me the loudest.

You will hear things no one else is hearing. I can also show you things no one else knows that is taking place around them. Their ears do not hear nor do their eyes see the shift I AM making in your world.

Don't try to explain to others because they won't listen. Instead, you look and listen for Me. There are laws of nature that I established, and there are laws of the supernatural that I enforce. No one and no power can override what I cause to happen.

Before I fill you with My presence and power, you must empty yourself. That's why you feel empty. I AM ridding you of those things that you have filled yourself with. If you give Me only a little room in your life, then there is very little I can work with. That's why you will see only very little difference.

Then you wonder why I AM not doing much in your life. Be emptied in order to be filled. Be submissive by giving Me more of yourself. Be open and don't be fearful. Feel My warmth for the moment even though you may not see any light. I AM with you all the way.

March 23

There are times you don't receive because you do not believe. Your thoughts are more about a God of the past instead of My present presence. When you gather to worship, My Word is sometimes read as a history about Me. My power has not diminished over time and neither has My presence.

Speak about Me and speak to Me where I AM. I AM with you this very moment. This does not confine Me because I was before time came into existence.

I see the past, the present, and the future at the same time. I know what is happening now in your life. I know where I can take you if you give Me that freedom to move in your life and in your circumstances.

It does Me no good to withhold what I have for you and it doesn't benefit you. Why would you want to live without My blessings? You have a choice every day and each day's blessings are not the same. They are for that day. Tomorrow will not be the same and that's why you are no longer able to receive yesterday's blessings once that day has passed.

I have for you what you need this very moment. Don't walk away from it because you lack the faith. All I need from you right now is just a mustard seed size of faith. Watch what I can do with a small amount. Then give Me more of your faith and see how much more I can do tomorrow.

March 24

You did not choose Me, but I chose you. You made the decision to respond to My calling on your life. My plans are the means to fulfill My purpose for creating you. I didn't create you and then later make a decision about what to do with you.

Your gifting matches the purpose for your time on earth. You were born for such a time as this. No other era would have allowed you to do what waits to be done.

A day delayed is a day unfilled. An opportunity was missed. A potentially changed life was left unchanged. Don't look at what others can do for you. Do a deed of kindness in My name. Be different by making a difference. Make that choice to make a difference. That's why I chose you.

March 25

You made it through some very tough times in life. What you are currently experiencing is not as much an uphill battle you earlier faced. You don't think you can make it through as you did back then.

Others admired you for your tenacity and never give up mentality. Now you don't think you have the strength to make it to the other side. You can't stop in the middle and you are too far into it to turn back.

Set your sail and allow My heavenly breath to help you to the other side. You don't have to struggle as you did before. Just rest in Me more than ever before.

Earlier it was about the fight. This time it is about the faith. You must believe I will see you through. This time the victory will be greater, but with less effort.

March 26

Anxiety is not from Me, but rather moves you away from Me. Peace is what sustains you through life, but is lacking in most of My children. I won't give you a scorpion, but will give you a fish. One brings death and the other brings life. Life comes from Me, not only to live, but to live above and beyond what you currently experience.

Never allow anxiety or fear to enter your mind. That only brings about the forces of evil and darkness, and it gives the enemy a stronghold. It can only cause darker shadows and covers light. Anxiety grows into fear which limits your faith.

Rejoice this day in Me because it is from Me. Don't let it go by and not receive My blessings I have for you. Believe in no other but Me. Believe that you can do all things through Me. And then watch and see what I can do, even with a faith the size of a mustard seed.

March 27

You are not to bow under the pressure of burdens you experience in life. You were not made to carry such a load. Neither were you created to live life the way you have experienced it. My yoke allows you to walk alongside of Me each day. No matter what you go through, I AM there with you.

The river never gets too deep or the mountains too steep that you will not make it to the other side. You will as long as you walk in My path. I know each step and the direction for each day.

What you went through yesterday brought you to where you are today. That put you in the place for you to experience a special blessing needed at this time in your life.

I know you won't give up. You've never done that before and it is not the time to do it now. Watch and pray. The next move will take you to a better place where you can serve Me the best. You will see I was there all the time.

March 28

You say you trust Me, but your faith wavers. It ebbs and flows like the never ceasing waves of the ocean. I remain the same and there is no change in My glory and purpose for creation.

You were made to have a continuous communion with Me. I AM always here for you and you can get as close to Me as you desire.

I have a love for you that cannot be understood by the finite mind because My love goes beyond your capacity to even comprehend. I gave to you the most precious possession—My Son. You say you love Me, but what has that love cost you?

Little cost means little sacrifice. Those who love Me the most are the ones who paid the highest price. The more you know Me, the more you will love Me and be able to accept My love.

A love for Me is how life is to be lived. I first loved you and desire to be loved by you. Make this day one of receiving My love, regardless of how you see yourself and how others feel about you.

My love overcomes any sin you've committed, any thoughts that turned sinful, and any deed that was wrong. Love Me where you are because I know who you are. Allow My love to capture you and bring a change in you.

March 29

You only go as far as your faith allows. You see only as far as your faith extends in front of you. I have more blessings for you and more places to take you if you will only trust Me more.

Life's pathway is cluttered with beliefs that only took believers so far. They chose to pursue Me no longer because they gave up on Me and themselves. A walk with Me should not stop before the end. The farther you travel, the more you can see what I've been doing all along.

There is more for you because I AM a much more God. You have to believe there is more than what you are experiencing, because there is more. Your faith is what taps into My reservoir of blessings. When nothing stands between your faith and My most for you, then is when you will have an overflow beyond your comprehension.

You are as much to Me as any created being. I didn't create you for no reason nor randomly. Allow Me to have more of your faith and trust and see what comes this very day.

Let My peace encompass all your thoughts and your future. I will be there for you when you arrive, just as I AM with you today while on the way.

March 30

Don't try to understand My grace. Just receive it and apply it to your mind and your life. It's needed and there for you. Grace is given out of love and My love covers all your sins.

It applies to your limited faith you have and it doesn't limit My grace. My grace is as unlimited as My love is unconditional.

You may feel you've lost much time in this race of life. It's not how you start, but how you finish. I will give you enough time to finish the race well if you dedicate the remainder of your life as a follower and not withhold anything from Me. I can give you more than you will ever be able to give to Me.

Another day of doubt will only cause another day of delay. Be set free of your fears by believing in Me. Faith and fear cannot abide together. Whatever you choose to dwell on will demonstrate itself in your walk and talk in life.

The more I AM a part of you, the more I can impart My unlimited supply of blessings. Make this a time to believe and you'll see an overflow of grace and unconditional love from Me to you. It's waiting for your willingness to ask and believe.

March 31

I AM crowded out of your life by your thinking. Your thoughts become engulfed by doubts and fear. As negative as that can affect you, it's still a part of you. There is more to life than just existing.

It's about Me and not just what you think about Me. I AM more than your thoughts. I AM beyond your ability to understand Me.

To move forward, you must go back to the faith of a child. It's just a simple act of believing. Believe without asking for an explanation.

Don't use an excuse to stay where you are. If you have no desire, then you have no faith. Make a turn and move toward Me. Shadows of doubt can become a part of your past and no longer bind you to the present.

Lay down every encumbrance that hinders you. Move with grace as you move with Me in your mind. Meditate on what I have done for you and expect nothing in return. Then you can see how great I AM and how great you can become in My kingdom's work.

April 1

You have toiled diligently without seeing the fruit of your labor. It doesn't mean your work is in vain, but rather a delay in the harvest.

It took the seed longer to die in the ground. It was longer before you finally died to your selfish desires and worldly ambition. You were dead in your desire to make Me the Ruler of your life. I was not to rule over you, but to abide in you.

Once you made Me your reason for living, then is when you began to live. Those have not been wasted days, but waiting days. You remained faithful in your pursuit of Me, even during those days when your heart seemed dead to anything spiritual. I never gave up on you and I know you will never give up on Me.

Live today alive. Be conscious of My presence and My leading. I AM directing your steps to a higher level which will give you a new dimension of My goodness and mercy toward you. I will show you My favor as you see showers of blessings that will soon come your way.

April 2

You view life as if you're still in the wilderness. Don't look at your surroundings. Look at Me. I AM the One who can remove any obstacle facing you today. Don't let it become a hindrance. Allow it to become a miracle in your life as I remove it from your path.

Living each day with Me can become better or bitter. It's how you choose to face it and how much faith you have in Me.

I AM unlimited in My power and strength. Creation was created with My words. It took no effort on My part. Your dilemma can be annihilated by a thought from Me. Don't look at the odds against you as overwhelming. See them as an opportunity for you to demonstrate your faith in Me. That's what pleases Me.

It's not about your accomplishments, but about how you choose to believe in Me and what you believe about Me.

A miracle can be easily demonstrated through your faith. Just choose to believe in Me and trust Me. Believe that I want the best for you and I will give you the best.

Life can be lived at a higher level than you currently experience. Trust Me on this one. Watch what I AM about to do. It's not a time to give up. It's a time to go on.

April 3

When you feel life is bringing you down, think of My Son when He was lifted up on a rugged cross. He didn't die for you to live with no life. He died so you could live abundantly and eternally in My presence.

My Spirit lives within you to give you joy and peace. My children should not experience anything less. Desire more of Me so you can live more for Me.

Be willing to move forward in life in order to follow Me, even if it initially feels like a risk. Faith must be the order of the day in order to pursue Me.

Staying in the boat calls for no risk. Stepping out on the water is where you'll find Me. Those who seek Me will find Me. Listen for My voice. The best for you is still ahead.

April 4

Be still and know. That's how you can learn more of Me and about yourself. My desire is for you to know Me so well that nothing can overtake you or cause you despair. Allow My love to overwhelm you, rather than the storms of life, to bring about stability and certainty.

Nothing is more important than time alone with Me. Set it aside and I will show you how I've set you aside to do My kingdom work. It's not about making a name for yourself, but making Me known to others.

You must have something to share with them, something they desire. That desire is to be about pursing Me. As you pursue Me, I will bring the plans I have for you into reality. They will no longer be things you chase after, but about My love that chases you down.

April 5

I brought you to where you are for a reason. It's not that you woke up one day and found yourself there. It's because I brought you here for such a time as this. My kingdom shall come on this earth. It comes into the hearts of My people. Open your heart to Me and see what I can do for you and through you.

I use earthen vessels to hold the good news and tidings of great joy to others. Let your life so shine that it draws others to Me. Set yourself apart by being a part of My kingdom's work on earth.

Let the world see you as different because of the difference I AM making in your life. It's not about a one time encounter. It's about God encounters, a continuing encounter and interaction with Me. Be holy, for I AM holy. Be all about Me. Let no opportunity slip away from sharing My love and your story with others.

April 6

You look for something to be different in your life each day. The difference is Me and what I have made you into. You are a chosen vessel that I pour My love and My life into daily. I AM there with you to help you make it through the storms of life. Not every day is a storm. When things are peaceful, know My peace and experience it.

I sent the Holy Spirit who gives you that wonderful peace and sense of contentment. Don't worry about upcoming things that may cause you to worry. Prepare yourself by being at peace with Me.

Nothing is greater than My peace within you. Dwell on it. Immerse yourself in it and let your mind be at perfect peace.

April 7

Be the standard bearer of a life filled with My presence and My Spirit. Let others see Me in you. That's how I make Myself known to many other people. Once you tell them about Me, they can experience Me in a way they never have known before.

It's more than just your requests while in My presence. It's about you giving Me the worship and praise I desire. I delight in that. That's what I want from you.

Make the time to give Me your adoration and praise. That's the reason for your creation, to be loved and to give Me love in return. Sing unto Me a song from your heart and I will give you the desires of your heart.

April 8

You committed yourself to Me when you didn't know what commitment was all about. But you did it because you wanted Me to be a part of your life. I want to be more than just a part of it. I want you to be all about Me.

When you allow Me to be that to you, then is when you'll become even more committed to Me. I have more for you than you ever conceived. Why? Because I AM totally committed to you.

April 9

Falling down is not a failure. The journey toward Me is full of many steps, but it also has its share of missteps. Mistakes are part of life, but the main thing is growing into the beautiful creation I designed you to become.

A butterfly must crawl through the dust as a caterpillar before it can soar into the beautiful sky. A child will have scraped knees before walking becomes natural. Don't be hard on yourself. After all, I loved you before you ever knew of My love for you. Love yourself through your mistakes and when you fall down. I do. So can you.

April 10

I left you My peace before I left this earth. I didn't take it away from you. Neither are you to let anyone else take it away. No one can take away what they did not give to you. Peace is what you need to make it until you are with Me.

Stake your claim today and let no one victimize you of what is rightfully yours. Do more than just possess it. Let My peace possess you and that will give you peace on earth. I left it for you and it is rightfully yours for the asking.

April 11

I heard your cries and remembered your pleas. You have not been forgotten, but will always be remembered. I have a place prepared for you because of all that you have been through. You still believe in Me, even when it seems there is nothing left to believe.

Stay on the straight and narrow and it will lead you to Me. Only then is when you can experience rest and understand the reason for your journey.

No chasm is too wide and no mountain is too high that can keep you from the love I have for you. Your journey will not be in vain. Listen to hear Me say one day, "Well done."

April 12

Joy should be your response in life. I created you and have sustained you. Another day on earth is when My presence abides in you. Have no fear about the future. Have a peace about the present.

I must do My work in you today so you can move on to tomorrow. Another day lived on earth is another day closer to being in My presence forever.

There will be no more questions. All will be understood when you see Me in all My glory. What you experience today will one day no longer be remembered. Forget the things of the past. You can't relive the past. You don't know the future.

Today is the day I have given you. Live it fully. Laugh along the way. Experience My joy I have for you being one of My children.

You bring Me delight. You bring Me joy. Now enjoy some of the joys of life that only come from Me. Count it all joy because all of that I AM doing in you and through you, even today.

April 13

Life cannot be lived all at one time. It must be experienced one day at a time. Once a day passes, it can never be recalled. Was it a day lived for Me? Or was it a day all about you?

I have more for you if you will make your life more about Me. I AM the reason for your existence and have allowed you to live for this day. It's not always about what I can do for you. Look and see what you have done for Me. I desire your love and your worship.

Praise is how you enter into My presence. No one can give you what I have for you. And only you can give Me what you have for Me. Offer up a sacrifice of praise. Let Me smell the aroma of your worship. Let Me hear how you delight in Me. I have more for you. Now, give Me more of you. Bring all your sacrifices of praise.

April 14

Today, let Me minister unto you. My Son took on your form and washed the disciples' feet with water. You are My disciple because you have been washed in the blood of My Son. It was a sign of humility.

I love you because of Him. Love Me because of My Son also. He showed you the way to Me. That is the only way you have access to My presence. Jesus showed His disciples how to humble themselves before others.

Offer your life as a sacrifice to Me. Live sacrificially before others. What will you offer that will always be remembered as something done in My name for someone else? My Son gave His life for you. What you have given for Me?

April 15

A memory is for remembering. The past is a remembrance. Think back how I revealed Myself and when I rescued you. You don't live in the past. It's only for reflection. Remember the good and look ahead to blessings yet to come your way.

You can't look ahead if you are looking back. You will only see what has passed you. See what I AM about to do for you. Unanswered prayers can still be answered. Dreams that haven't been fulfilled can still be in your future.

I can bring out the best in your situation and make it into a better future. What looks like a disaster may soon be realized as the best for you. I know what I want for you. I know how to get you there.

But you may not get there if you're unwilling to go there. And you can't more forward if you choose to remain in the past. Fold up your tent and look for the cloud to move.

April 16

You will hear Me in the stillness of the night. When alone and afraid, listen to Me speak to your spirit. You know My voice because you have obeyed Me in the past. A small voice can be heard when things have come to a standstill.

You don't know where to go. You don't know who to listen to. That's the time I sometimes finally speak.

I don't shout if you choose to listen to others voices in your thoughts or only look at your circumstances. It doesn't mean I AM not near if you don't hear Me. It simply means you choose to focus on other things and the mountain in front of you.

You don't have to shout and make a lot of noise about your circumstances. Listen more. Talk less. Look more to Me. Live more for Me. Others need to see Me working in you. They can't see Me if it's all about you. In order to increase in your life, you must decrease the way you try to control your own life and destiny.

April 17

You have much more to give to Me. It's not what I want from you, but what I have for you. You want a much more life and I have much more I want to give. You can't see Me if you're only looking at your circumstances.

Look up, for I AM above your circumstances. They don't pull Me down to your level, but I can lift you above them with Me if you learn to trust Me.

It's more than an occasional process. It is something that needs to be lived out every day with whatever comes your way.

Don't allow your circumstances to confuse you. You may have walked this way before, but I will take you to the other side. I know how far it is and I know the depth of the dark side along the way.

I will make a way and show you which way to go. Put your trust in Me and place your hand in Mine as I take you to the other side.

April 18

You have been in a valley of dry bones for a season. The air has become stilted with no life of any kind around you. It is My Spirit that I breathe into you to bring life. My breath gives you new beginnings and hope for tomorrow.

I can live through you that will draw others to Me. You have a certain calling for a certain period of time. Once you've waited for Me, then begin to move with Me as I move you into the realm of kingdom work I have designated for you.

Don't look at what others are doing in My name. Look at the areas where you have a desire to be about My business. You can better serve in the areas where you are better gifted. Use your gifts I have given you.

Go where you are equipped. Remain until I move you. Be patient and learn from Me as I now teach you even more things.

April 19

You may question your purpose in life, but don't question My existence. You will never be able to fathom all that I AM. I reveal only certain aspects of Myself to you. I do the same for others, but maybe a different attribute.

Revere that which I reveal to you. You will never know all of Me, but learn all you can about Me from what I've shown. Don't be dismayed because you don't know all you want to know about Me.

Be secure in what you know. Never let go, regardless of how much you still don't know. Guard what I've taught you. Teach others what you know. Share the good news. Once you choose to share, then I will reveal more to you about Me.

April 20

Don't focus on the speck in someone else's eye. It may be small to them, but you have made it big in your own logic. I am the Judge and no one can serve in that position but Me. I have My own way to deal with others who seem to stand in your way.

Before you can move forward with Me, see what is standing in the way between you and Me. You have enough troubles without making trouble with someone else. I see what needs to be done and I will see that it gets done.

April 21

I AM your source that can supply all your needs. I know what you need, even before you ask. But I want you to ask so you can see your supply comes from Me. If you don't make your request known to Me, then you will not know from where it came.

All good things come from Me. That's why they are called blessings. In order to be blessed, there must be a Blesser. I AM that One and I AM the One who has an unlimited supply.

I not only know what is best for you, but also when it is best. Trust My timing. Time will not run out on Me. Don't let it run out on you trusting Me.

April 22

My Son told you He would leave you with peace. But peace has sometimes left you. Your worry causes you to become uncertain and insecure. Be certain of your commitment. Be sure of your salvation. Be full of faith and grounded in truth.

There are many false doctrines and false teachers. They discern from only a finite mind. I have infinite wisdom. I will not deceive you. You can be deceived by those teachings not of Me and by teachers not from Me.

You can be sincere, but sincerely wrong. Test the spirits. Trust My Word. Allow Me to live through you. Then others will know where you are coming from and what you came through.

April 23

I AM not against you, but your enemies. They have entrenched themselves in your mind and plotted evil against you. Do not be slow in calling upon Me. I have made a way of escape.

The ransom has been given and paid by My Son with His own flesh and blood. The flesh is mortal, but the cleansing blood is for eternity. You have been saved and sealed. You have been called and commissioned. Do not hesitate to step out in faith.

Follow My voice and you will not be trapped. Obey My commands and you will not be captured. You can't see the end, but I can get you to the end. I will get you home.

April 24

Change blows in the wind. My kingdom moves forward to fulfill My purpose and plan for you. Don't resist the change I AM bringing about. It's not only for you, but for others. Be prepared to move forward, just as the children of Israel made a move each time the cloud moved.

The time frame may catch you camping instead of packing. Don't be weighed down with possessions. The one thing to take with you is a promise. My promise was made with you and it is for your good.

Give Me the freedom to bless you by trusting Me with your future. That's why you must move and be willing to accept change.

April 25

I not only hear your cries, but also see your circumstances. Your groans don't go without My awareness. You must go through a valley and climb the next mountain before you reach the next summit of your Christian journey.

Don't stop because that only delays the joy that awaits you. Joy comes with a better understanding of why I chose this path for you. You will understand it better by and by.

April 26

The path to My plan for your life is never straight. You sometimes must take detours that lead to darkness. But I will lead you through the dark nights. Light is always on the other side. There is an end to your present trial, but you must continue in order to reach the end.

Darkness always brings questions to your mind. But those questions can bring you to a fuller understanding about Me. Darkness can be deceptive. You may not see Me or even sense My presence. But it doesn't mean I don't know of your dilemma.

Darkness is as light to Me. Nothing darkens My understanding nor dims My view. Because I AM able to see, I AM able to know. Hold to My promise. Your hope is your lifeline. Never let go of that Blessed Hope, My Son. Put your hope in Him and I will see you through because of what He went through on earth.

April 27

I was there for you before. I will be there for you again. For the present, I want you to know My presence. My Spirit is in you. My angels surround you. Nothing will be able to come against you without My permission.

Testing is a part of life, even for Adam and Eve. I sometimes expose your weaknesses to you before the enemy exposes them to others. Allow Me to strengthen your foundation before a storm washes you back into discouragement or depression. A sure foundation must be built on My words that are recorded in My Word.

April 28

Do not fear the future. I AM already there when you get there. I have prepared a table for you to fellowship with Me. I desire to give you My love and receive your praise and worship in return.

You long for peace. I know how to get you there. Be still and listen to My voice speak to your spirit. I want you in My presence, just as you want My presence to be around you.

Come into My presence rejoicing. That is music to My ear and a sound that causes the enemy to retreat. Fill the air with rejoicing. I listen for your praise while you listen for My voice.

April 29

As the stars shine to signal My wonder, so should you be a light to others where My grace shines through. You may feel you are behind a cloud for the moment, but you may be the only light someone is seeing.

No matter how dim your world may seem, it is sometimes the only light to give hope and direction to a fellow traveler.

Your light is a reflection from a bigger source. Your source of light only comes from Me. Keep your life pure so My light can be seen even brighter.

Don't be a light in hiding, but one that is ever shining. Let someone see hope today while on your journey. You may be the last hope that person will see in a world that has become darkened and silent.

April 30

Life is about My salvation. Don't lose the joy of your salvation. I AM the One that brought it to you and am still with you. I have not deserted nor forsaken you. Allowing the enemy to speak otherwise is a day of joy you have lost with Me.

Your salvation is sealed, but your joy can be seized. When the enemy steals your thoughts, your joy is lessened.

What I give to you is meant for you and is to be a part of you. Your destiny is to Me and each day is a day closer to a life forever with Me. You know the way.

Now know the joy that is to accompany you today. It is available each day. Make it count for Me and that's how you can experience joy along the way.

May 1

Don't worry if you have taken the wrong path along the way. There are choices you must make each day. You may be at a detour that seems to be a dead end. You may be lost, but I know where to find you. You have never been absent from My sight and My presence will never leave you.

A wrong path can work for the good along the way. I can use your mistakes for you to see My mercy. Others can see your wayward walk as a way that shows them I AM truly The Way.

You may feel less used by Me through the wrong choices,

but there is something to be learned along the way. Once you learn, you won't have to travel that way again. Move along the path I place before you.

May 2

Success is not to be judged by the success of others. You are wonderfully made in My image and endowed with gifts specifically designed and given to you.

There are things you can do that no one else can. Someone may have the same gifting but cannot make the same journey in life. Each one has a different path for a different time frame.

Refusing to use your gifting is a refusal to recognize My handiwork in your life. Imagine the joy when you see how much you were made in My image and designed for this moment in your life. Seize the moment and use the opportunity before you to make a difference.

May 3

Your mind is a storehouse. Allow it to be filled with the goodness and mercy of My ways toward you. Life is filled with sorrow, but they are not to be stored. They serve only as a stepping stone toward Me and My help during those troubled times.

The storage tanks of your thoughts are for those needed reminders in life about My presence and My help. Keep them filled with what you want your future days to be filled with.

Bad grain brings no crops for tomorrow. Good grain can bring forth a bountiful harvest. Remember the good times. Recall from the past what you want Me to do again in the present.

What I have done, I can do again. What you need today,

I can supply this very moment. Remember the days of old. I can renew them once again.

May 4

You stand before Me with a bowed head and an open heart. You feel as though your hands are empty because of the little difference you think your life has made in the king-dom.

Don't think of yourself as someone whose worth is less than others. My Son died with the same amount of love for you as anyone else. You are not loved less, even if you some-times see yourself as unlovely.

Every path you traveled has been for a purpose. The times when the paths of others crossed your way were for a reason. I AM painting a beautiful mosaic of your life.

Each event adds its own colors to the landscape along life's journey. You are an earthen vessel, but you have an eter-nal treasure stored within you.

May 5

No one can remove the permanent purpose that formed your life at its inception. I knew your purpose before you ever knew My presence. The steps I ordained for you will be revealed. Trust is what you must have in Me for all that I have for you.

You cannot see My face and live. But you can see I have passed in your midst by the past blessings I bestowed upon you. Be confident of the future by placing your trust fully in Me.

May 6

You have laid up treasures in heaven, but I still have others hidden that you have yet to discover. I lead you there by My directions. You won't be able to uncover them until you arrive.

Don't stop yet, even if you think they will never be found. They were not placed randomly, but for the time they are to be discovered and uncovered.

Although you don't see anything around you or in front of you, I will direct you to that location. My directions will not lead you in the wrong direction. That will only come when you choose not to follow My directions.

May 7

I have not forsaken you. You have not been removed from My sight nor from My protective hand. You may see nothing, but I see everything. You are still being shaped and made into My image.

Don't try to make Me into your image. Your thinking can't even hold My thoughts. I know your future, even your future thoughts. I prepare the way as you make your way each day.

Don't look to others. Look to Me. I will take you where you need to be. I must get you there before you can move to the next step.

May 8

You can only see where you have been. You will recognize the future once you are there. When your future becomes your present, that's when I will do the things for that time. Until then, they will still remain in the future.

Experience Me today. Don't look to the future. You will be unable to see anything. Be a part of what I AM doing today. That's how you will know I AM doing a work in your life this very moment.

Don't try to draw strength for tomorrow. My supply is for today. Tomorrow's supply will be there tomorrow.

May 9

You have been saved for such a time as this. It is a time of difficulty, but also for victories. When you approach your Red Sea, do not be dismayed. It is there before you until the proper time for advancement and advancing the work of the kingdom.

The sun continues to shine, even behind the clouds of discouragement and confusion. When the light breaks through, you will already see the reason for the timing of crossing over to new land and new heights.

May 10

The wall sometimes seen in front of you is more than just for protection. It's also to keep you from seeing certain things surrounding you. When you see the spiritual warfare surrounding you, it will cause you to fear and not move forward.

I know when to reveal certain things surrounding you. It is usually after you have passed the test of trust and moved forward. There are certain battles that only the forces of light can fight.

My angels keep continuous watch over you. They move at My command to protect you from annihilation. When you cannot see, it is for your good. Be thankful for My protection and your limited vision.

May 11

Leaning on your own understanding will eventually lead to a collapse of life itself. Limited understanding brings about limited vision. Limited vision does not allow you to see the bigger picture of your life and life itself.

You are to walk in fullness and that comes when you fully trust in My infinite understanding. You only know what you know and see now. Fragments are not the whole, only a portion. There is a reason and a time for each move I have you to make.

My movements allow you to see more. Seeing more allows you to see more of Me and a better understanding of where you have been. Follow Me to experience the fullness of life and to the finality of My plans for you.

May 12

Waves are caused by winds above and currents below. Both are invisible. It's the invisible that drives your life. Forces of evil and good are not visible. It's when you arrive that you can finally see which one moved your life along its path.

My direction for you is for the best. The way is more difficult than anticipated, but I will bring you into the harbor of safety and peace.

Peace not only will come at the end, but can come while traveling the journey of life. Peace is not just an end result, but can be a companion. Experience it along the way. It allows life to have more meaning and the storms seem less violent.

Pick up the garment of peace and wrap it around you for protection from the storms of uncertainty.

May 13

You were given the breath of life at birth. You have received the Breath of Life of the Holy Spirit at your spiritual birth. Breathe in the truth of Me to better know Me and to know yourself.

Outside of Me you are nothing. All of your life is to be about Me because eternity is how long you will be in My presence.

Know Me better and you will learn more about yourself and your reason for being. When I breathed life into you, I also instilled a purpose. The meaning of life is about Me. How often you try to live life without Me. I AM your reason for being. Learn from Me and live for Me. There is nothing outside of Me.

There is more to life than you know because of your limited knowledge about Me and My ways. Move forward with anticipation. Know there is more to life and more about Me than you've ever known before. The more you learn, the more you can live in truth and experience My favor.

May 14

The more you give of yourself to Me, the more I can give of Myself to you. I look for those who see truth and are willing to live in it. Not all can handle the truth, and I have only given what you can handle.

Live life in total abandonment and I will fill your life with My presence. The fear you have about what others may say will only limit what I have to say to you. More truth comes with a total abandonment for Me.

The areas of life you never released to Me are areas that I will not reveal Myself. When you pursue Me completely is when My work that I began in you can be completed. Knowing Me is the greatest thing you will ever know.

May 15

I sometimes hide My face for a while. It's for you to know more about yourself and to see yourself as I see you. My hiddenness exposes your inwardness. It allows you to see who you are and your thoughts about Me.

Is truth or doubt revealed? Does trust or disobedience come forth? That's when you can see yourself as I see you.

The revelation of My presence will again be revealed. Walk in the light I set before you once again. The more you see of yourself, the more I will show you of Myself. You become more aware of the light once you've stood in darkness.

My Son had darkness to come over Him, but in the end He chose to trust Me. You have that choice before you. Will you trust and believe what I promised earlier?

It lies in your future, but first you have to encounter some darkness. I will be with you so you will not be in total darkness, even if everything seems to be dark all around you.

May 16

The way for you doesn't seem very clear, but I have cleared the way and you will soon see what I have done and prepared for you. To get to the other side of the dark forest, you must go through it. I AM with you as you go, and will also be waiting for you on the other side. I do so because of My ever present presence.

You are not alone. Others around you are going through some of their darkest moments, even darker than your present moment. Look around you and not just for Me. Give help to someone who is hurting. They want to receive help from Me and many times My words come through other messengers.

You are mine and can carry a word of encouragement to others. Let them see you are looking up and not down on what has you down. Walk alongside someone during troubling times like the two on the Emmaus Road. My presence was with both of them at the same time and will do the same for you.

May 17

You can hear Me more in silence. That's when you feel alone, even in the middle of chaos. Things may be quiet all around you, but not in your mind.

Thoughts cascade as a roaring waterfall. The noise of trouble drowns out any solitude. Listen in silence. Be still and listen to My still and quiet voice that speaks to your heart and mind.

You look for a sign, but you fail to listen. If you know Me, then you will know My voice. You heard Me when you invited Me into your world. Listen once more and you will hear again.

What I have to say needs to be heard by you. Redeem your time and give some back to Me. Call upon Me and I will answer you, even in silence.

May 18

A fire is hot. You know that. But you don't know how hot it is until you experience it. To follow Me, you must go through a refiner's fire. That's when you know the real cost of following Me. Impurities must be burned away before you can stand before Me as a pure vessel.

Many impurities don't need to be seen and spread around to others. Others need to see your purity and holiness in order to see you being used to do My kingdom's work on earth.

In order to see the final product, one will experience varying degrees of heat and intensity while in the refiner's fire. I see your heart and your motives. I know when the last speck of foreign matter is in your life and mind. That flaw can be an entry point for the enemy to bring in more impure thinking and unacceptable deeds.

You will not be removed until those things not of Me are burned away. I will not leave you too long, but know the moment you are to be removed from the fire. Removing you too early will only cause more brokenness, more remolding, and more fire.

Stay until I remove you. Then is when you will see I was there all the time and better understand the difficulties and heartaches that came your way.

May 19

You are My beloved and I take joy in you believing in Me. You may not sense My love and presence, but both are with you. They have been there before you were created. More of it will be made known to you when you know and experience more of Me.

Let no one convince you that I AM not present and choose to do nothing in your life. I work through all things and can cause them to bring you into My presence more than ever before.

I know what I want done in your life and know how to bring it about. You can either trust Me or turn away from Me. There is no middle ground.

I AM against your enemies. I laugh at their plans for you. I can make them flee in a word. Don't be afraid of them and don't fear them. Stand in My strength and commit your ways unto Me. I will show you My way as you walk in truth and in My light. See what I AM about to do.

May 20

I entrusted My plans to you, but sometimes you don't trust Me to bring about those plans. Things in life can work for your good and thereby bring about some good things in your life.

Life is difficult with the cross you are to carry while following Me. The cross may be seen as humiliating, but it also can bring humility. You are to humble yourself before Me, and many times it is by way of a cross.

Although others may think you brought it upon yourself and you may not understand it, the reason for the cross and the choosing of you are part of My plan.

Don't walk away from what I have called you to do. My calling has always been upon you. Others may not see it. You may not sense it, but it is there. Although the plan was formulated from the beginning, it is sometimes not finalized until the very end. You have not yet reached the end. Your calling still remains.

Trust Me as I entrusted to you My calling on your life. It's not you calling. It's Me that has called you. That call comes with a calling. Trust Me for it, just as I have trusted you with it.

May 21

Mistakes in life can be a milestone instead of a millstone. A millstone weighs you down and can take you into the depths of despair. It can drag you down in life and become a distraction.

A milestone is a reference point that can turn you toward Me and in the direction of a more promising life than originally experienced. All things can work for the good in life, even a mistake. Let Me turn it into good and see a more positive outcome.

Mistakes were made by My first created beings. Your last

mistake won't be your last one. Turn to Me and watch Me turn it from a millstone to a milestone.

Learning from an event or decision may cause you to never have to pass that way again. Live and learn. That will help you to better understand Me and My purpose for your life.

May 22

I have begun a good work in you and it continues even this day. The latter days will be better than the former because of the way My Spirit will be poured out on you.

The days of struggles were not in vain. Neither are they over. Total and sweet victory will come once death has been conquered and you are in My presence forever. While you are on earth, My Spirit is there with you to assure the deliverance of you to Me at a designated time.

Today, I will order your steps once again. Each time you put a foot down, you are conquering new land and entering into a closer presence with Me. Do not turn back, but choose to move forward and advance My kingdom on earth. There is where you will experience My presence and see My mighty hand at work more than ever before.

May 23

You will never know the future, but I do. You don't know My plans, but you will soon. You do have a promise from Me. I promise never to forget you nor forsake you. I have more for you if you will trust Me more.

Trust is when you see nothing in front of you, but can see what I have done behind you. You live in the present and that's where I make Myself known to you. This is a day I have made. I brought it into existence with you still existing for it.

Make the most of it by making Me the most important One in your life. You may have to forsake others and forego your immediate dreams for something bigger that I have for you. Keep your eyes on Me as you move toward a new horizon where blessings do await you. They are from Me, so come to Me, and do not turn aside or around.

May 24

My children hear My voice. You heard My voice and heeded the call. That's why you are on this journey and the reason I AM moving you onward and upward. Each step should draw you closer to Me and better understanding of who I AM.

You may have questions, but you shouldn't continue the questioning of Me. I AM who I AM, regardless of your thinking. You know someone if you know their heart. Know My heart and My love for you. Then you will know Me better and a better understand My ways.

May 25

"Who do you say that I am?" That was a question My Son asked His disciples. That is the question I ask you today. How you answer is for you, not for Me. I know your thoughts. But you must face your thoughts and doubts about Me.

I sometimes choose to limit My response when you limit your faith. No one who puts their faith in Me had too much faith. Your faith can't supersede My power. Your limitations limit your faith.

Plant that simple mustard seed of faith once again. Simply believe and only believe in Me. That's all you need and that's all I need from you. Add that childlike faith to your thinking and watch My blessings multiply.

May 26

Let the day be a day of trust, even in the midst of turmoil. I knew the outcome, even before it began with you. Life is not easy and can sometimes be very hard. I can make it bearable because of My Son who bore the cross and was buried in the tomb for you.

He made the way for you to make the way for others. They listen for the words you speak when there seems to be no end to your suffering. Do you want pity from others or praise from Me?

Let your actions speak on behalf of your beliefs. Don't give up hope. Believe in Me during this time and you will receive your reward that waits for you.

May 27

When you question Me, you want answers. When you doubt Me, you limit My endearment. No one can take My place and neither can anyone take the place of you. I designed you with uniqueness and you are an original.

Receive My thoughts with your mind. Allow your heart to contain My love. No one can take My place and neither can anyone take your place. I dwell in you like I do with no one else. My life in you makes you unique. Be the one who shares My love with others like no one else can do.

May 28

In time you will know all about what will be made known. In the meantime, you will only know what I choose to reveal. That's all you need to know. Trust Me even when your knowledge is limited and your sight hindered. That's where trust comes in. That's when you need to become totally dependent upon Me.

Don't try to understand what I don't make known. Don't try to go where I've blocked your path. Don't try to speak unless I have given you something to say. Silence, sometimes, can say a lot.

Trust in Me with all your heart and you will lack for nothing you need. I AM the Provider who brings things into existence by speaking a mere word. But My words are mighty. Darkness flees at the command of My voice.

Be ready when the call comes, regardless of the season of life. My calling gives you a reason for living each season. Follow through to the end.

May 29

You know My Word, but you don't fully trust Me for My works you think I should be working in your life. You know what I can do because I have made Myself known. I revealed Myself earlier when you called upon Me.

I change not. I AM the same today as I was yesterday. Nothing has become harder for Me. You have experienced hard times and life will continue to have difficult steps. But I AM there with you.

Your trust should be building instead of collapsing. The only way it will collapse is if you build your faith on man's belief system. But you believe in Me. I AM that solid foundation upon where your hope lies.

Trust Me this day. I will take care of tomorrow when it arrives. Don't worry about tomorrow. I AM already there also. I simply ask you for a simple trust in Me.

May 30

I have strengthened you in the past and will be your strength today. Without Me, things would be impossible. All things, yes all things, are possible through Me. Your faith is to be used for such a time as this.

You may not see where you are going, but I will see to it that you arrive at your predetermined destination. Your life will extend into tomorrow. When you arrive, I will already be there.

Now is the time to know that I AM causing all things to work together for your good and My glory. When you finally enter into My presence, you will do so with praise and thanksgiving.

My Spirit will be your guide and will lead you into those hidden truths that will be revealed to you at the designated time. Trust Me like you've never trusted before as I take you through times you have not seen before.

You will not be alone. I will be ahead of you, with you and even behind you as you journey into My fullness.

May 31

Do not be afraid of tomorrow. I have already prepared a place for you. Even though enemies may surround you, they will neither touch you nor deceive you if you stay in communion with Me.

I will reveal before the enemy can expose. I will bring to light what was hiding in darkness. I will be a shield also around you from the fiery darts and the traps Satan has in place for you.

I have a place for you, but you must first arrive before you can be put in place. There is where you will serve Me with the gifts I placed in you.

Be joyous on this journey. Don't allow the enemy to rob you of your joy or steal the precious memories of the past. More joy and soon to be made wonderful memories are just over the horizon.

June 1

You have served Me well. I knew your heart when pursuing Me and I knew it while you were imprisoned in your world. You have journeyed a difficult path that has no directional signs.

But I kept you on the right path, one that was less traveled. That gave you more time with Me. I heard your silent prayers. I saw the tears of loneliness when you thought no one understood you.

Darkness will give way to light, especially the light that now shines in your life. You had to be hidden before you could be seen. You were humbled and that brought humility to your walk.

Live in the light I now provide. Look at silence as sacred. See the new horizon before you. You will now see what I saw all along. You will understand it when I make it known to you.

Let nothing discourage you. Feel the warmth of My love and know I AM with you always, even to the end of this life and beyond.

June 2

Uncertainty brings about anxiety and worry. Neither of these are from Me. Where I AM about to take you will be absent of these negative implications. You will see all that I AM doing and what you do is for a reason.

Life is not about happenstance or those things that happen for no particular reason. If so, that will mean I have no control.

Don't be looking for something that may not be there. At one time you had more trust in Me. I have not changed. Only your trust in Me is no longer the same.

You should be more trusting of Me because of what I have

already brought you through. You made it thus far, and it was not just on your own. It was Me then. It will be Me again.

June 3

Every day is a miracle from Me. The air you breathe and the flow of blood within you is from Me. That sustains you and allows you to partake in even greater miracles.

Faithfulness is what I look for, especially during those times when your heart is troubled and you see no way out of your circumstances.

I AM above your circumstances, and yet know every intricate detail of your difficulty. I know all of those things in order to make all things work for the good in your life. I don't just use the things that you are aware of, but also those things which you never see or hear in the natural.

What I did yesterday in your life was to bring about a change for today and even tomorrow. You forget so quickly of earlier deliverances. Why do you not believe I can do the same today for you?

Anxiety and lack of trust will only cause the delay of your deliverance. Use today as a step up and on to other things instead of dwelling on the present dilemma. Give Me praise for your upcoming deliverance.

June 4

Today is your Red Sea Crossing day. You have come to what seems to be the end. The enemy still barks at your heels. You can run no faster and you can run no longer.

Don't mistake My miracle as a stroke of luck. It's not about luck or how things happen by accident. There is a certainty in every move that I make.

I made a move earlier in your life that brought you to this

place. Now as I make a move, watch and see what I can do for those who believe. I believe in you. Is it too hard to believe on Me?

You believed earlier and it set you on this journey. Believe even more while on this journey. Because it is not over, there is still time for more miracles.

Stand back as I prepare the way. Walk into the fullness of My Spirit and your new possessions.

June 5

You will always be My child. Now you must become My warrior. The battle is ever present and it will intensify. My presence must become more present and it comes through My people.

Many feel they have lost the battle and have not yet begun to fight. Don't give up before ever beginning. Each new day the enemy can have a different strategy.

Be on battle alert every moment. Go about what I called you to do, but don't become less convinced of your surroundings. See what I AM doing, but also see what the enemy is trying to do.

The enemy won't retreat if victory is in sight. That's why you need to see what I AM doing and what you are not allowing Me to do. You invited the enemy into your mind. Now remove him from your thoughts and think about Me.

June 6

Even though your plans for life seem to be on hold, I continue to hold you in the palm of My hand. It is there where you are protected. I have you where you need to be for the moment. Anything outside of Me is not of Me, neither is it from Me.

You may not know the way for the moment, but I will direct your steps to eternity with Me. Tomorrow is unknown, but you know Me. That is all you need to know.

Don't look at what you may lose, but what you can gain if you trust Me. The best can still be ahead if you fulfill My plan set in motion before you were ever created.

You can only see as far as the horizon. I made the horizon and I made you. I can take you to the place where you can best serve Me. But you must be willing to go beyond the unknown. To stay where you are is to settle. People who settle become part of a settlement. They choose to go no farther.

There is more because I have allowed you to live this long. If you stop here, you too, will become a settler. The yearning inside of you to live more fully and freely for Me is the pioneer spirit placed within you before I placed you on earth.

I AM in front of you, showing you there is more life to live. Don't become lost among the masses. You will end up no different than any of those who lost their way along the way. Choose to become a part of Me by setting yourself apart from those around you.

June 7

I know all there is to know, that was known, and will ever be known. Yet you sometimes think you know all about certain circumstances and dilemmas you currently face.

To be limited in your knowledge is to be limited in your understanding. I already know your future because it has already been known to Me.

It is better for you for Me to know what lies ahead. That is why I send you through the necessary preparation stages even though you don't think what I AM doing seems to be necessary. It is for your good and for all the upcoming things to work out for your good.

June 8

My hand is on you and has never been removed, even during your lonely days when you thought your cries went unanswered. Weeping is the sound I hear that causes a pause. I stand beside you and allow nothing to come your way that would destroy or divert you.

You were competitive, but now you are compassionate. Your heart searches for Me. Your eyes look for Me. I can be seen around you when you search your surroundings and your world.

I AM there with you. Nothing can separate My love for you. Neither will I ever allow you to become separated from Me. How can I leave you if I will always be with you?

June 9

Your desperate situations are a delight for Me. It allows you to experience My unseen hand at times when you think I AM nowhere around. I can make the impossible become possible. Look at such circumstances as a way to look for Me and the exercise of My power and authority.

Nothing is impossible for Me. You please Me when you exercise your faith. Look for Me, especially in those desperate situations. That's when you know I AM the Deliverer, the One who will make a way. Know Me. Know My ways. Then I will show you the way.

June 10

Forgiveness is an ever present reality. No actual act or unseen thought is too big or too evil not to forgive. I know your sins, even before they become known to you. All has been covered by the blood of My most precious Son. Don't allow guilt or past sins to be a stronghold on your pursuit of Me.

I loved you before you even knew Me. I continue to love you, even after your most present sin. And My love will be there for you when you commit your last one on earth. Have the mind of Christ Jesus who lived sinless while on earth.

Pursue Me even more and you will sin even less. The bride of Christ will be spotless that My Son will present to Me. Be a part of My kingdom on earth and you will enter My gates with thanksgiving.

June 11

I AM with you in those lowly places. No place is so low that I cannot reach down and make known My presence. You will never be so alone that I AM unable to make My presence known.

Seek My face. Pursue Me. I will make My presence known at the time you are to know. Remember the past when I rescued you and brought you safely through those violent storms. I did not allow you to drown. You are still here and I AM still with you.

Dwell on My love for you and My assurance that My presence is present in you. There is no need to see if I can see your struggles. I know them. I have allowed them. I will see you safely through and then you will see the reason for such a time.

June 12

Your journey brought you to this present place. You would have never known My love for you if you never made it to this place. My presence has been revealed more prominently and powerfully in deserts, in storms, in prisons, in pits, and even in the most painful persecutions.

Know I AM with you. Know that I will see you through. Know that I will never leave you, even when darkness seems to be all around you.

Joy will come in the morning when the light of My presence reveals the reason for these dark nights. You will see how I brought you through. And when you go through it again, I will do it again. I will never fail nor forsake you. Look for Me today, for I will make Myself known.

June 13

Someday you will understand My words to you and the life I called you to live. You cannot relive today after it has passed. Neither can you live for tomorrow because it has not yet arrived. Be at peace in the present. Be content for the moment.

I bring peace, but I also bring a sword. You will be protected when confusion reigns all around you. You will know My presence by the peace in you. It will be a peaceful presence.

June 14

Death is a doorway. It will be locked for no one, but will be opened for everyone. Do not dread its approach and do not fear what is on the other side. If you accepted My Son on earth, He will be there to accept you into My presence. Don't let doubts deny your presence.

June 15

Go with the flow of My Spirit that flows within you. Be filled and be aware. I speak at times in a whisper and during total silence. Look for Me in things around you, but listen to what I AM speaking inside of you. Be in communion with your spirit to My Spirit. They are not to be in conflict, but flow together.

June 16

Do not disregard the lessons you learned in the past. You not only learned them, but they are lessons for today. The first occurrence was painful, but not to apply it today will only cause more pain.

Lessons are not just for learning, but for living out. Learn from Me each day and live for Me every day.

June 17

I heard your cries, even before creation. I knew of your dilemmas, even before it was created. There was a solution in place, even before the situation arrived.

Trust Me for this time in your life. There is a reason for this season. It must be experienced before you move into the next realm of My instruction and blessing.

I will complete that which I began. The end is not yet because there is more to come, both in instruction and movement. You are not yet where you need to be, but I AM moving you in that direction.

Trust is what you need the most. Trust Me and see what I will do for you. You are the one I have chosen for such a time as this. Your reward is forthcoming and will soon be before you.

June 18

The way seems impossible. The path looks insurmountable. The darkness makes it seem impassible. But I know the way through. I will lead you gently and carefully.

You cannot turn back because you've come too far. The distance is longer behind you and will cause you to not receive the reward ahead of you. It is yours to claim and will be given to no one else.

Faith has brought you this far and will lead you home. That is where I await for you. I see clearly the steps to be taken. Trust Me more than ever before for the remainder of your journey. I AM with you along the way and will take you all the way home.

June 19

You don't know where to place your hope, but you know who to place it in. It is in Me, not only the Blessed Hope, but your Blessed Hope. Nothing in life is eternal or self-sustaining. Mountains erode, glaciers melt, rain falls, and plants die. But the hope in Me can last forever.

Do not be dismayed by visible signs or outward conditions. All matter rests in Me. I AM the Alpha and the Omega, not only the beginning and end of life on earth, but also your present life. All of life is at My beckoning. Events can turn simply on My thoughts.

Be at peace with what I have said. I AM in control and all things are subject to Me. I AM the Overcomer and will help you overcome this difficulty in life if you trust Me.

June 20

Joy is the heartstrings that play a melody for Me. I rejoice in your joy and that's the way I created you. You were made to experience joy within and to express joy to Me. When joy flows from your heart, it flows into My presence.

You want Me to hear your prayers and I want to hear

your praise. Be thankful this very moment that I AM with you. I brought you to this point and there is still more of the journey yet to go.

Joy does come in the morning. There is light just beyond your present darkness.

June 21

Abandoned is a thought that only comes from the enemy. At times, I will be silent, but I will never abandon you. You sense My presence on the mountaintop, but I AM also with you in the valleys of life. That is where you can learn more about Me and My ways.

Remain faithful when things fall apart around you. I AM aware of those times and events also. You will one day look back and see those not only as growing times, but also when I was gracious to you and brought you through. I will never leave My children. No, not ever.

June 22

My sufficiency is made known through your insufficiency. My strength gives you the needed strength during your times of weakness.

There is no need to look for others to help you since My Spirit is your Helper. He is all you need. Do not look beyond what is inside of you. That is where I dwell to help you do your best.

I AM the Giver of life who gave you life in the beginning. I also will be the one to determine how long you will have life. You have more life to live if you live for Me today as you have never lived before. Remain faithful to Me as long as life remains in you.

June 23

Give no thought about how your needs of tomorrow will be met. That is My part to fulfill. You must remember that all good things come from Me. No one knows you any better and no one can provide any better than Me.

I do not want to see you in need when it is Me that can meet all your needs. Why trust others today when they can be gone tomorrow? Trust is all you may have left to give Me. That is all I need and that is how I can fulfill all your needs. Trust Me today, for there really is no other way.

June 24

Be mindful that your insignificance to others is of no significance to Me. You are a precious jewel that I purchased with the life of My Son. That's how precious you are to Me. That is how much I love you.

Questioning My love for you is an insult to Me because I paid the highest price anyone could ever pay for you. You are worth more than you will ever know. Make your life worthwhile and worth living for Me.

June 25

Do not be afraid of your future. It has not yet arrived and you know nothing about it. Why worry over something that is not yet known? I know your future and I have no worry. Your future rests in My hands and that future to you is not yet known.

Allow Me to move you to the place in life where you belong. Let Me place My protection around you and more of My love in you. I will take you where you need to be in the future. Go with Me and put your trust in Me all the way home.

June 26

If you give up on life, you have given up on Me. You were not created to quit, but to continue on this journey to the end that I determined. I know where and how this will end for you.

Stopping short will result in unreceived blessings. My blessings do no good to stay with Me. I created them to be released at certain times. But you must be willing to receive at that time.

Don't let Me and yourself down. Listen to Me to tell you where to go. Then walk in it and receive what is waiting on you.

June 27

Don't measure your life by the standard of others. They are not the standard of measure, for they will also be measured. I determine where each person is to be placed. I knew your potential and placed you accordingly.

Where you are planted is where you are to bring forth fruit for Me and others to see. This cannot be done in the wrong place at the wrong time. All has been done for you to bring out the greatest potential that can yield the greatest productivity. I set the standard and that's how you are measured.

June 28

Nothing you will ever say or do will change My love for you. But be mindful of what comes to your mind. Thoughts lead to action. And actions are what others see. What they see in you is sometimes a reflection of the way they see Me.

I AM a God who sees all and knows all. Nothing has been known or will ever be known that I do not already know. No one knows better than Me and that is why it is best for you to know more about Me.

June 29

I remind you of My goodness, but you seem to focus on your sorrow and trials. Thinking about such events cause dark clouds to cover the way I AM preparing for you.

In order to get to the next place, you must journey through this place for the moment. It may seem like an eternity, but lasts only as long as I deem necessary.

Put the days behind you that have already passed. Don't keep them in front of you, for they only cause doubt and discouragement. The past is gone and will no longer return.

Make the day one where you bless My holy name. By doing so, you will be blessed in My name.

June 30

Life is more than what you create in your mind. It's about Me, the Creator of the universe and all things that are created. Your life is more than how you see it even now.

Limited thinking disallows the limitless possibilities I can bring about. See life through the eyes of My Son. Look for ways to share My life and bless others. His time was spent with the outcasts and those outside the religious circles.

When you extend mercy, that is an extension of Me through you, touching the essence of life. Make your life about Me today. Reach out and touch someone who needs a touch from Me.

July 1

Mistakes are made and they are also forgiven. Living for Me does not bring about perfection, but it can bring about peace. Rest in My love for you. A wrongdoing doesn't cause Me to love you less, but it will allow Me to show you how much I love you.

Don't allow continued guilt to rule you when I have removed your sins from you. Be thankful for the new day I give you to experience My love for you in a new way again.

July 2

Look for Me each day. Listen to what I have to say. My presence is never away from you, but all around you. I know your ways. I even know them when they are only thoughts in your mind.

What you do or say never comes as a surprise to Me. You can never catch Me off guard or Me not know something that is not yet known. I know you. I know all about you.

Allow Me to take you by the hand today as you journey to the Land of Promise. Blessings can be experienced, even before you arrive. Let Me guide your thoughts today.

Allow Me to give direction when you seem unable to move. When there seems to be no way out of your circumstances, I will make a way. You trusted Me in the past. Trust Me even now.

July 3

Life will not always be lived. Live what life you have left for Me. It's not something that you plan to do in the future. You live in the present, so live it specifically for Me. It's not about what you can become, but who you are in Me, even for the moment.

You are surrounded by a cloud of witnesses who made it to the end. Don't give up or give in. You have more life to live and I have more blessings for you. Don't give them up by giving up.

I AM with you always, and always also means now. Open your heart to My love and your mind to My way of thinking.

July 4

Never am I absent from your presence, even when you no longer say I AM no longer near. I have never left you, so why do you act at times as if I AM not making Myself known? You can never escape My presence and you will never be left alone.

I know your needs and when you need Me. You worry instead of worship. You panic instead of praying.

Don't be afraid of stepping out on faith. That's when I step in. Faith is what sets you apart. Be a part of doing My kingdom's work by doing what I've set you apart to do.

July 5

You are called by Me and set apart from others. You long for Me, but I also long for your love. I made you in such a way to have an everlasting love for Me. It's up to you to exercise that love and a freedom to express it.

Let it be known by your life and the way you live it. Be so much in love with Me that nothing else matters. Why do you not express your love to Me after all the ways I have loved you?

Fill your cup with My love until it overflows. I have so much more of My love to give if you will only receive it. There is nothing you can do to earn it, but only to receive it.

Once you've tasted My love, nothing else will ever satisfy that desire. Drink of My love that has been poured into you.

July 6

I will replace what you have lost in your pursuit of Me. Do not look with sadness what was given up in My name. Much more will come your way that restores what was taken away.

I don't look upon it as something that can't be restored. There are better things and more to be restored than what you originally possessed.

I know what you had and I know what I have for you. I do not replace with less, but restore with more. Don't look at what you don't have, but what you do have and also what I promised in My Word.

If I looked after a nation of My people in the desert, can I not look after you during this dry season of your life?

July 7

Many of your nights became sleepless and many of your days turned into restlessness. You knew of My presence, but didn't know what I was doing. It was not for you to know, but now I AM beginning to let you know.

There was not a day that passed or a test that was failed that I didn't know about. I saw you then and I see you now.

You can't reach higher ground without a climb involved. You struggled mightily, but I kept you from falling. I extended My hand when you needed it the most. Lift up your head as I lift you up to a new level of My presence and blessings to you.

July 8

Oh, My child. How I long for you to know how much I love you. Your past sins did not keep Me from accepting you.

Neither will your present failures prohibit you from entering My presence.

The blood of My Son covered all of your wrongdoing. Nothing said or done will change My relationship with you. I love you that much.

Can you not love Me more since there is no more I can do to show you any more love? Wrap yourself in My love and don't be deceived by the enemy's lies.

July 9

None of the righteous go begging for bread. So why do you sometimes have that mentality of Me being unable to meet your needs? It is not because of a lack of supply on My part, but a lack of faith in Me on your part.

I did not call you out, only for you to have to beg. I called you to be a blessing to Me and to bless others.

You are My holy instrument to play a melody of praise. You are also the instrument of My hope and love to others who don't know of these things.

Be an instrument, not a beggar. Exemplify the life others want to live, not one they turn away from because of your lack of trust in Me.

July 10

As you serve Me faithfully, the attention and the focus will be on Me. That is what your life is to be about. Direct all praise to Me and I will direct My blessings to you. It's not the container that is to be the focus, but rather the content.

Be filled with My Spirit. Make it a desire to live fully for Me each day. You will be filled beyond measure and others will experience the overflow. They will be blessed as I bless you with the anointing of My Holy Spirit.

July 11

Do not think it is strange that you have been set aside as a chosen vessel. My message is contained in earthen vessels. You look at the distractions and the discouragement that continuously come your way.

The instrument may be cracked, but not broken. It may be chipped, but it can still contain. Others forget the simplicity and scars etched on the container when they see what the container is holding.

It is a sweet wine of My love that touches the lips of wandering strangers in a wasteland. They come to you for the content and not the container.

The more simple the container, the less focus it will be. That is why I call you to a simple lifestyle, so things will be about Me and less attention to you. Be passionate and exemplify purity on a daily basis.

July 12

No one can know Me like you do. No one has been through what you went through. I did not leave you alone, but brought you alone to Me. Others will not experience what life has been like for you, but you can help them experience Me by exercising your faith and following Me the remaining days of your life.

Some don't see a lot of Me because they choose to see less of Me. They are comfortable with Me not taking control of their lives. They don't want to go the way I chose for them. It was a choice they didn't make. The road for them is wide because there are many who chose that way.

Your way is narrow and many think you are too narrow minded. The way is narrow that leads to Me and abundant living. It doesn't need to be wide because few travel this way.

Abundant living is now for you and abundant riches

await you also. They are for you because of the way you chose to follow Me.

July 13

Joy is found within you because that is where I make My dwelling place. Where I AM welcome is where joy abounds.

Be at peace so I can reveal My presence and My purpose for you. You cannot hear if you are not in a position to listen. Be focused on Me, and less on the things that are distractions. Let this day be one of hope and peace, a day for later reflection and not one of regret.

July 14

Enjoy My presence. Along with My presence comes peace. With peace comes purpose. I gave you a promise that I would neither forsake you nor leave you. I did neither one.

You are where you are by My own choosing. You do have choices in life, but you asked Me to take control. You chose to let Me control. My control takes you where I want you to go.

Make the choice again today to allow Me to direct your path and keep you in the right direction. For the moment, things may not seem right. But I will make things right for as long as you trust Me.

July 15

Once your journey begins, it moves you forward. You may not determine the pace or the path, but I work all those things for the good. What you consider good may not be good for the moment.

But My good is for the best. There is nothing better than

the best. My plans include the best for you. Those plans will be fulfilled as long as you continue to follow Me.

July 16

Peace on earth is important, but peace within you is most important. Peace comes to those who trust Me. Peace with Me can bring peace to your surroundings. Allow others to sense My peace through you for this day.

Tomorrow has enough troubles of its own. You don't need to borrow from tomorrow. I will already be there, but for this day, I remain with you in your present situation. Allow My peace to permeate your mind and spirit this very moment.

July 17

You chose earlier to follow Me. You continue to believe I have more life for you to live. These next moments are from Me and they are for you. Let no one steal your joy that can be yours.

I only need your willingness to trust Me. A lack of trust results in a lack of peace. I AM here for you, to rescue you from the pit of depression and discouragement. Those are pitfalls from the enemy.

The more you fall into his traps, the longer the time it takes to experience what I want you to have from Me. Missteps result in missed opportunities. Make your goal one that moves you toward Me and away from the enemy's traps.

July 18

My presence is present with you at this very moment. I don't leave you and return later. I never left you and have always remained with you.

Be not afraid of what is ahead. As I remain with you, I AM also ahead of you preparing the way.

When you feel abandoned, it is only because of your thoughts being open to the enemy. He will influence you only as long as you entertain him in your thoughts.

Guard your mind by reminding yourself that Christ is in you. Have the mind of Christ and that allows My Spirit to influence and direct you, not only your thoughts, but also the way you should go.

July 19

Don't worry about the length of your life on earth. Life is only a vapor on this earth. As soon as you know life, you will soon no longer live here. I have a better place for you. No more worries, anxieties, mistakes, hurt, or loneliness.

You will be fulfilled when living in My presence. I don't save you just for you to see a shadow of Me. I came to earth so you will be in My presence forevermore.

I desire you to be with Me. I made a way before there was ever a way for you to dwell with Me forever. Why worry about temporary things that will no longer be with you? I have more for you than you can ever fathom. All that you need will be given to you in full measure.

July 20

Step forward today in My light and My love. You will see and sense them. I have so much more because I AM not a God of Scarcity. Those who see Me that way have formulated that concept of Me in their thinking. That is the way many have come to see Me. But that is not the way I would have it.

I made Myself known to you. I will reveal more if you make Me known to others in everyday life.

Life is more than deadlines or dilemmas, or those devastating disasters that have crushed you. I AM the God of Peace and Purpose. I do what I do for a purpose. It can affect people, or even one person.

My purpose is enveloped in My presence. When My purpose is being fulfilled, that's when you sense My presence. Nothing is done without Me knowing. My knowledge is part of My presence. Do as I direct your way and you will find My peace in your presence.

July 21

Don't try to know all things because you will never know everything. I AM a multi-faceted God and I only reveal in part at certain times. Go with what I have given you. Look for revelation as I reveal more of Myself to you.

You do not need to know if it is not time to know. Knowing all leaves no room for faith. Trust is the connecting point. Believe Me and trust Me. That is all you need for this moment. Look for more revelation as I reveal more of Myself to you.

July 22

It's not how others see you, but how I see you. I see all because I know all. Others don't see because they don't know. Others' opinions of you are not your concerns because that is a choice they make.

Don't try to make them change their minds. Just be mindful of Me and make your life all about Me.

I AM the One who matters. Make your choices about Me and you will be less concerned about how others think of you.

July 23

My world is bigger than your world. My world is unable to contain Me, while your world contains you.

Don't be limited by what you can do when I have unlimited power that can work through you. Nothing restrains Me, but your thinking sometimes limits what I can do in your world.

People struggle because they don't know what I want to do in them. They focus on their limitations and forget about My power to overcome their obstacles before them. See Me as One who can see you through your trials. No formula, just faith.

July 24

Some day you will only be a faded memory to others. To Me, you will be in My presence forever. You were made to experience My love and mercy. The hurt from others will only last for this lifetime.

But after that, you will have no more painful memories. You wonder if life will always be hurtful. Don't be overwhelmed by the pain. Think of the time you will one day have with Me. And oh, what a time that will be.

July 25

Hard times make it hard to rejoice. But they won't last forever. That is something in which you can rejoice. Even the greatest leaders who sought Me did so in times of conflict and chaos. That is why they became more aware of My presence than ever before.

Look for Me in the small things. That is when you will see a glimpse of My glory. It's during those sightings that you can know I still dwell in your presence and I AM with you.

Those glimpses are not to be by accident, but ordained for such a time as this. Look for Me in all things and you will see what I AM bringing about in your life.

July 26

Let not your heart be troubled. You were not made to have a troubled heart, but a trusting heart. Trust is what I placed in you when I entrusted you with the plan I have for your life.

Your purpose has not yet been completed and that is why you remain. Trust Me because I know what plans I have for you. I can do more for you today than what you can do for yourself in a lifetime.

Don't bypass the blessings by bypassing My plan for you today. Listen to what I say and see what I have for you coming your way.

July 27

Others don't see the way I do. Their ways are not your ways. My way is one I designed with you in mind. No one can live your life better than you. You have been designed with a special destiny in mind.

Don't desire the life that some live. Instead, believe that I have made you to be a part of something bigger. My plan for you includes My kingdom on earth as it is in heaven. It's here for you to experience now and not just later.

July 28

You have seen Me operate in the bigger elements of life and the balance of nature. I also work in areas not seen by man. In your life I orchestrated your essence in life. I have for you a responsible task for completion before you finalize your work on earth.

What you thought was in vain will now become visible to others as a work I chose you to do. Little was thought by the many around you. They could not see My work, but only what they deemed as mistakes and misdirection on your part.

There was more to it than was seen by others. I was doing a work that was unknown and unseen. The seed has to die before a sprout comes to life. What I did is now being brought forth.

You will now see the sunshine that was hidden for much of your life. My light now provides the warmth needed for My tender love you now experience.

July 29

For a long time you were somewhat fearful of the future. You future is now, for I now do that work in you for which you were created. No fear, only know Me. Replace your fear with the faith you were created to have in Me.

Faith brings into being those past dreams. It also brings about the blessings awaiting your arrival on those days in the future.

Release them with your faith and know they come from Me. Know Me more and you will receive even more.

July 30

You will make it safely home. I have a hedge around you and My plans for your life. They can't be taken away from you, but you are the only one that can fulfill them.

Don't allow the enemy to destroy what I have in place for you. He not only wants to destroy your plans, but also you.

A little can be costly, but the battles in My name are worth the cost. Great is your reward in heaven. Lay up treasures in heaven, the ones that come through trials on earth.

Forge ahead, but do so with a fighting and victorious faith. The end is not over until it is over. Don't stop or come to a halt when there is more than ever before. Seek Me now and more treasure will be stored up for your arrival in My presence.

July 31

Calm is part of My doing. As the waves were calmed for the disciples, I can also calm your storms. There seems to be no way out when looking all around you. I AM not only in your storm, but I AM also outside of it.

I know where the sun is shining and when the clouds dissipate. You can go into the darkest part of the storm if you refuse My direction.

Strengthen your courage and face the howling winds and darkened skies in My strength. They are no match for Me, the One who not only controls them, but also created them.

I also created you to have unsurpassed strength and unfailing faith when you believe in Me with everything within you.

August 1

Be kind to each other. Grow in My strength and My love. Judgment is to be left to Me. You are not to judge others, but to serve Me daily. The way to serve someone is to come into their presence.

You are not only to come into My presence, but to do so with thanksgiving. Give thanks with a grateful heart. Let your gratitude be known about Me, not only to Me, but to all.

You enjoy the times when gratitude is heaped upon you. You were made to express your love to Me because of the love

I have for you.

My Son died for you because of the love for you. Can you not love us in return? Do you have to be reminded?

Give thanks with each breath you take. Even that is from Me. Be grateful because I have so much more to give.

August 2

Do not be afraid to go into this coming day. I AM already there. I will not just watch from a distance, but will move into the day with you. As I go, I have already arrived. I will be there to meet you.

Nothing is unknown to Me. Your questions have already been answered. Seek My face and I will share what you need to know. All will not be made known because of your finite mind's inability to know all things.

I give you the capacity to receive what you need to know. Trust Me in all things, even the things that I have not made known to you.

Allow a trial to be a turning point for you. Good can come out of the upcoming situation. I can make all things work for your good, even when everyone around you sees it as bad.

August 3

Your failures are magnified before others. They see what they want to see and not what I see. You are a diamond being cut and shaped into the image of My Son.

You are priceless, but you have been purchased with a price. My Son is precious to Me, and I presented Him at no cost to you.

Yet not allowing Him to become part of your life is costly, more than you want to pay. It will not only cost your life, but also your future. Turning over your future to Me will turn out to be the best for you.

When I AM all that you have left, you will then see it is all you need. I AM the one who can meet your needs at all times. Prove Me and know you will never prove Me wrong.

August 4

You deserve peace so much. I have more than you can ever desire or will ever need. I don't withhold to make it worse on you. My peace is to always be with you. You don't experience it because you allow your thoughts and worry to extract it from your mind.

When you have the mind of Christ, My peace is imbedded. Jesus experienced My peace in each calm and crisis moment.

My peace is there with you. You don't need to wait on it. You ask for it, but it is already there. Don't ask for it. Acknowledge that it is there with you. Now accept it into your thoughts.

Demonstrate it in every situation and every conversation. Do it now and see how My peace can change your thoughts and your situation. It changes chaos into calmness and helplessness into hope.

August 5

Your future is tomorrow and that is where it is to stay. You can't return to yesterday. Neither can you move into tomorrow while today's light is still shining. Walk in the light, the heavenly light that shines from above to light your present path.

You can see all that needs to be seen. You will know what I make known to you if you live this day for Me. Rest in My presence while I restore your soul.

I will return what the enemy has taken. My promise is still good. Your hope lies within Me. Those who don't know

Me don't know what I have for them because they chose to turn to their own way.

You have turned your heart to Me and I will never turn My back on you. And you will never be alone. Not ever.

August 6

Hardships can either harden you toward Me or help you face the extreme hardships in life with the faith that can outlast the most difficult circumstances. You can face today because of what you endured yesterday.

Don't relive the difficulty life brought upon you in your mind. Remember you came through and that allows you to stand in triumph today.

You weathered the storms, survived the wilderness, fought the enemy, and that now allows you to claim the victory in the name of holy God.

Look for those who continue to struggle. Make yourself available to others by standing beside them and keeping their arms raised.

You came through to the other side. Help someone make it to the other side by not leaving them until victory has been secured.

August 7

Where you are today is no accident. Neither is it your final resting place. You have a spirit of restlessness in you that urges you to keep moving forward. The final prize will not be given until the final end.

If you turn back now, you are turning away from the blessings that await you. No one can receive what I have just for you. No one can appreciate what you have endured in life more than you. No one will be able to be as grateful for what I have designed and designated more than you.

The greater the price, the greater will be the appreciation. When you experience those showers of blessings, you won't have to be told, "Give thanks." Your thanks will ease the memory and pain that have accompanied you up to this point in life. It will be worth it all. You will know when you see.

August 8

My child, you long to hear My voice today. I speak when you need to hear, so be listening at all times. I will not withhold anything that needs to be said if you are listening to My voice.

Calm your soul, then listen and look for Me. Be aware of what is happening today as I prepare you for tomorrow. What you hear today will be needed to discern My direction for tomorrow.

I AM guiding you today in order to be aligned for the place you need to be tomorrow. Don't cause a delay by allowing your thoughts to be influenced by the enemy's influence. The longer you listen to him, the more familiar his voice will become to you.

I don't condemn My children, but chasten and comfort them. Wrap yourself in My love and be still as I speak in a still small voice.

August 9

You dismiss the needs of others when you are in need. You will be encouraged by Me when you encourage others. Needs are met as you address the needs of those around you. Do not look for others to do what you want Me to do for you.

Investing in others multiplies what I give you in return. One who builds bigger barns in order to hoard will soon have their barns emptied. I give, but I also take away. The wealth of this world is Mine.

Man owns nothing permanently. All will die at some point. More will be shared when you share more. Practice what I told you to do about the poor.

August 10

Discouragement can easily bring about defeat. I continued to encourage My servant, David, even with the number of victories he accumulated. Determination in My name replaces the discouragement the enemy tries to bury you under.

The more he heaps, the more you become helpless when you don't fully exercise the faith that is deeply embedded in you. It was given to you for such a time as this.

Let your faith rise above the doubt and discouragement. Let it soar to the forefront of your mind and your thinking. Faith pleases Me. It brings a smile to My face and it lifts My helping hand to be extended to you.

August 11

Doubt delays My plans. Discouragement drowns out My voice to you. You choose who to listen to and what message to believe.

I know about your dilemma and I see your circumstances. There are opportunities along with the obstacles. Each situation is either a stepping stone or a stumbling block.

Move up to another realm of spiritual awareness. Allow your ears to become more attentive and your eyes more alert to the circumstances you face each day.

You may panic for a moment, but allow My peace to enter and to endure. Your biggest and longest struggle is hardly more than a fleeting moment compared to the life of eternity you will spend in My presence. It will be worth it all when you see the worthiness I see in you.

August 12

You are a friend to Jesus who has made you part of My family. A family reunion is posted on the calendar for the time each one is invited. Some already arrived and are waiting your arrival.

My Son will be there to welcome you. Others will gather around Him when He announces your arrival. The hardships will be replaced with happiness. Joy will fill the air. Laughter will be heard throughout the streets.

You wait for My Son's return while others wait for your arrival. Your place is prepared and heaven can hardly wait. Believing this allows you to bear it a little longer while you await your departure.

August 13

You know where you have been in life and I know that too. But I also know where you are going, something you don't know. I know the distance yet to be traveled, but I also know the time it will take for you to make it through.

Shelters are already in place along the way. Each one is strategically placed that will provide rest and nourishment. The journey causes one to become weary and thirsty. It was the same for My Son.

He needed rest and meals along the way. My Beloved spent time with Me for long periods of time in order to be prepared. His life was too tough for most to follow. Only those who committed their lives for the kingdom were able to see it through.

Their discipline helped them become disciples. Be committed to My calling. Be confident today and you will see the way while on the way.

August 14

I trust you, so don't break your trust with Me. Miracles were performed on your behalf you didn't know. You didn't know it was My Spirit intervening on your behalf. No one can provide for you better than Me.

So trust Me in everything and for everything. Others may seem to have the answers, but don't know what needs to be known in order to provide. My resources are limitless.

Don't be limited by your faith. Have faith in Me. I will direct your steps and ordain your thoughts for a new and better way. Trust Me with today.

August 15

Your future with Me is still bright, even though your words and doubts seem to cast a cloud over what lies ahead. Those clouds do not block My view of you. Don't allow them to block what I have in store for you.

You will always make mistakes and say things out of order. Forgive yourself, just as I forgive you. My love for you never changes. It does not diminish based upon your thoughts of Me.

I have My plans in place. Trust Me for what you need. I will do that and even more. The more comes from an alignment of your faith. Align it with My potential and see how much more I can do.

August 16

No one loves you like I do. No one understands your concerns better than Me. Your worry doesn't solve, but adds weight to your already weighed down soul. I AM your burden bearer.

Cast your concerns, worries, and negative thoughts on

Me. I don't retain them. Instead, they are released and sent to the abyss. Now rise up and walk with Me.

Look ahead to the land of redemption. That is where all that has been lost will now be restored. Punish yourself no more. Enjoy the bounty of blessings set on the table before you today.

August 17

Don't turn back or turn away because you think you disqualified yourself. No sin is too great and no wrong thing is so wrong that it cannot be covered by My love and forgiveness.

My love for you includes My forgiveness of you. Dwell on My goodness and mercy. That follows you all the days of your life. It doesn't begin tomorrow. It includes today.

August 18

Life is filled with My goodness. Be mindful of My blessings each day. It wasn't made to enjoy only when you arrive into My presence. Life is to be lived here and now, to its fullest.

Take in all that I place before you. Renew the new way of perceiving Me. Set aside the old perceptions and walk in the newness of what is being revealed. A new walk includes a new way of thinking.

Don't punish yourself. Be pure in heart, for you shall see Me. That includes how I will lift you today out of the pit and into My presence that can be seen all around you.

August 19

Life can be more meaningful if you allow Me to help you

more. You carry the same burdens for too long, the ones that you no longer should be bearing. Forgiveness is the key to unloading them at the foot of the cross where My forgiveness was demonstrated openly for all to see.

Remove encumbrances that beset you and run the race with vigor and purpose. Life is not to be lived aimlessly and with no meaning. You have a reason to live. It is to receive My love and demonstrate it to others.

Make the most of where you are because tomorrow you may be in another place for another purpose. When the day ends, there will be no more time to complete what is needed to be lived out.

Make peace by placing yourself under the blood of My Son that washed away your sins. Allow Me to restore the joy of your salvation and the hope that comes from Me. You don't live life alone. I AM with you and will help you in whatever way you need to lead you home.

August 20

"Be still and know." When you are still, you can know Me in the silence. You want Me to work actively in your life. What you experience many days is chaos and confusion. I AM neither of them. My presence is revealed in the stillness of the soul.

I desire your entry into My presence. But you must be still before you can know. Set aside the time or otherwise I will have to set you aside through circumstances. I work in all things, so why not choose the silence and retreat from your world?

The land is dry where you reside. Drink from the spiritual fountain of wisdom that you are nearing. Take in the water and the manna that awaits you. Know that your needs will always be met when you meet Me in the stillness of your soul.

August 21

Speak to others as I speak to you. Be the voice in the wilderness where those around you continue to wander. They know Me, but they don't know My voice. Not being in relationship with Me often brings silence.

Be still. Know Me. Hear Me. What I say is not always just for you. Certain ones spoke My message to you earlier when speaking about Me. That was a way you came to know Me and more about My ways.

You listen for Me when you think I AM speaking through one of My followers. Be the one willing to be open as an instrument to carry My message. Don't consider your unworthiness, but your usefulness in My kingdom.

August 22

I AM your strength for this day. I will be there for your tomorrow. You will not have a day without My presence. When you seek Me, don't be afraid that I won't be there. As you are more mindful of My presence, the more I will make Myself known to you.

You don't have to move back into the valley of uncertainty as long as you know for certain that I AM here. Don't give back any land to the enemy. You are on a mission and My command is to continue forward. Do walk in peace, for I have the way prepared and your steps ordered.

August 23

I came to you in Spirit, and My Spirit is Truth. My word never returns void, but brings about My purpose. Today is not a day for wandering, but is a day where you will see My hand on your life.

No move is outside My view. I not only see you, but what

you are seeing. Just because you see it, it doesn't mean it is from Me. You must know Me if you are to know what are My ways.

For the moment, be silent so you can sense My peace. The more you experience My peace, the more you will know Me. Worries about tomorrow do not provide solutions. They only cloud your mind, resulting in more confusion.

Rid your mind of worry so today won't be just another day. Make it one where you rejoice in all things.

August 24

Walk with Me this day. I set it aside to make Myself known to you in a way you want to know Me. It's not just about where you want to be in life, but where I have you for this moment.

You need to be here in order to move you where blessings await you. They will come upon you as a shower. As you feel rain, so shall you feel My presence and My peace.

You are here for Me. I have you in this place and around the people I place around you. You want to see Me, but they do also.

Allow My presence and My peace to be seen in you. They will know I AM with you. Tell them of My love and what I have brought you through. Tell it to anyone who will listen.

August 25

There is peace in the valley. You can find it there as you pass through the shadows. You do not walk it alone, but I AM with you.

You have gone through each valley that was before you. You made it to the other side. My peace was with you then, so be at peace now. You don't have to look for it when it is with you, even now.

Distractions come from the enemy. Don't go in that direction. Turmoil is not from Me, but I know when you are in it. I can use it to bring you into a closer relationship with Me and into a deeper meaning to life. You will see how all this works together for your good and My glory.

August 26

Rest in Me as I give you the rest that surpasses all understanding. Your prayer didn't fall on a deaf ear. I heard your cries in the night of your soul, even when there was light around you. You will never walk in total darkness as My light lets you see the path. The entire path is not illuminated, but enough for you to see the next steps.

August 27

You have more of the journey left because you have not reached the end. Though the future may seem bare, I AM already there. Though darkness seems to be all around, you will be shown the way.

You need to be here today to get you where you need to be tomorrow. This is not your final place. You may rest along the way, but you cannot make this your final resting place on earth. There is more time left in your life and that means more road to travel.

Don't focus on your physical condition, but on your spiritual condition. I can bring others to you when you can't go to them. I will make a way for what needs to be made known.

I will show you the way because I AM the way. It will be made known to you because it is the way I would have you go, so walk in it.

August 28

Do not wrestle with the worries of this world. You need My peace through the storm, not more worry. Worry allows more clouds of uncertainty to gather. Clouds block out the sun which gives warmth and the ability to see clearly what is around you.

As you look around, you will see Me working in you and guiding you through what surrounds you. It's a simple command I give, "Follow Me." If that's all you hear, that's all you need to know.

August 29

I make delays and detours to your day without you knowing it is Me. I have a reason for all that I do because it is in your best interest.

I know all things and you must learn to trust Me in all things, even if it looks like I AM not involved. You are special to Me and it's during these times when you can learn more about Me and My ways.

One day you will better understand, but until then, I can make this situation work out for the best.

August 30

Stay close to Me. Lay your head on Me, like John did to My Son, and hear the beat of My heart. By doing so, you will feel and sense My love for you. I show it every day, even when you don't sense My presence.

I have you here today in order to move you into another realm of living for Me. Don't be content where you are because there is more living to be lived, more lessons to be learned, and more blessings coming your way.

Showers will eventually cease and clouds move on to another location. At some point, blessings will cease where you are. You must move with the cloud, just as My children moved about in the wilderness.

Each day I will provide until I move you into the Land of Provision where My bounty abounds.

August 31

Know Me this day more than ever. I reveal more of Myself to those who pursue Me. It's about relationship and not rituals. I choose to reveal less about Myself the more you try to control the events in your own life.

Never try to travel this journey alone. Even My Son was guided by My Spirit. That is what you need also. My Son left so the Spirit would come upon you. Listen to My voice. Obey My command. Make every day count for Me.

September 1

Life comes and life goes. You don't know when you will be called home. So live today as if it is your last day on earth. Others can see more of Me when you dwell in peace and not be worried about tomorrow.

Today is not to be skipped, but to be a stepping stone for your next step toward a higher plane. I will lift you if you are willing to be led.

Don't be disappointed today if it has been one of discouragement or disaster. You had to go through it in order for Me to move you forward. Don't stop here. Don't stay here.

Life has not come to an end even though the enemy wants you to think it has come to an end. He cannot make that call because it was Me that called you into being when I created you.

September 2

As you experience peace, you know it is from Me. It is a peace that bypasses your mind and is sent from above to dwell inside you. Allow it to permeate the way you see circumstances in your life.

I was there when you entered them and I AM there as you go through them. I will also be there after you pass through so you can see it was Me who helped you through.

Approach the future with confidence and a contagious faith so you can give inspiration to others. There were those who inspired you at the beginning of your journey.

Now you are to be an inspiration to those who are beginning the same journey you began when you started fully pursuing Me.

September 3

Let others see Jesus in you. Actions speak louder than words. You will be able to share more once they have seen more of your walk with Me. You can't outlast My love. You can't outrun My presence. I will always be with you.

Look for Me in the hours and days ahead. You will see more of Me than ever before. That's what I desire from you, a desire to see Me more than ever before.

September 4

The world will see more persecution of those who follow Me all the remaining days of their lives. Those who suffer for My name's sake will be remembered on Judgment Day.

Your sufferings will be made known to those who didn't know you. All will know what was said and done to you privately. Only I know when you suffered in silence.

Don't seek a reward or recognition by promoting yourself

as a martyr. They will see the mental lashes and emotional scars delivered by your enemies.

The days of your suffering will be made known to those that questioned your obedience to Me. They didn't think I would put you through the suffering you encountered.

It was Me and soon they will have to admit you followed Me all along and all the way through.

September 5

Doubt and discouragement are stones that cause you to stumble and snares that entangle you. They serve as a way to slow you down or shut you down. They can cause you to take your eyes off the prize and find yourself in a pit.

The pit of self pity causes you to look at your dilemma and not what I AM doing in the middle of your circumstances.

Setbacks are only temporary. My call on your life is permanent and without repentance. You grew in faith as I helped you through. I AM your deliverance from whatever is placed before you by the Adversary. Be thankful for what I brought you through. Give thanks for upcoming blessings because of your faithfulness.

September 6

Watch how others begin to see you as I have begun to show them things in the spiritual realm. The journey up the mountain of life has been difficult. The floor of the valley brought silence and loneliness.

What I saw you through is what others will now see. Your journey was not without falls, but you never failed Me. You followed Me. There were times that made little sense. But I knew you would make it through.

This is not the end, but more is to come. You will experience more blessings, a greater capacity to accept more of My love, and a better understanding of your journey.

September 7

When you allow worry to occupy your mind, there is less room for My peace. Many things occupy your mind, but you can only think one thought at a time.

Worry can lead to disillusionment and even a downfall. But My Spirit can lift you up and take you to new heights of a peace that can surpass your dream of what that would be like.

My peace brings calmness in the middle of your storms. The disciples' storms calmed when they called upon My Son. Call upon Me and the storm will move on.

Don't get drenched in discouragement and anxiety. That only comes from the enemy, and only at the times when you entertain his thoughts in your mind. Have the mind of Christ and have My peace that can be yours by believing in Me and My words I speak to your mind.

September 8

No one can outrun My love. It surrounds you and covers you with a covering that will never disintegrate. I made your mind, but I also gave you the choice of determining what to fill your mind with.

Accepting My love can bring about a greater acceptance of yourself. You must first love yourself before you can love others. Loving others, but seeing yourself as unlovely because of your lack of trust in Me, is not lovely.

That is not the way I would have it. I created you to love yourself, just as I love you. I have forgiven you, so forgive yourself.

A lack of trust causes a loss in your day that could be pleasant and peaceful, even in uncertain times. I know where I want you to go and I know how to get you there.

Allow My Spirit to guide you, but let My peace permeate your mind. There is nothing greater than My peace and there is nothing that it cannot overtake.

September 9

A gift can be a surprise until you unwrap it. My love for you may take you by surprise when you see and feel what it is really like. It's not something just to be admired, but something you are to accept from Me.

I do not ask for it back. I only ask that you see it as a gift from Me and something that can become your most treasured gift.

The world didn't give it to you and it can't take it away. Only you can refuse to acknowledge it is from Me and live a life without fully experiencing it. When you see how My love can bring you joy, it also brings joy to Me.

I can laugh at your enemies and scorn them. I can also laugh with delight when you see the joy of accepting My love for you. It gives you something you were meant to have and made especially for you.

I love the unlovely and the unwanted. That is who My Son ministered to while living among you. Love them as I have loved you. You can never go wrong by giving My love to others. That pleases Me and can bring peace to you.

September 10

No one can love Me the way you do because of the way I made you. You were made to be a recipient of My love, but also a carrier. Take it with you wherever you go. Don't store it, but share it. Be a conduit through which love flows.

Be the one that someone else can sense My presence in, even the ones who question My love or even My existence

Put on the garment of praise and sing with joy for what I AM bringing about in your life. Have the joy down in your heart so it can spring up like a well.

Be sensitive to My presence. Be open to the things from Me. And be ready to show My love to others at all times.

September 11

I will never forsake you nor leave you. You felt abandonment from Me, but that was not from Me. The enemy wants you to think I gave up on you for you to give up on Me. Even if you did, you can choose this day to change the way you approach Me and think about Me.

Have lovely thoughts about Me because of the way I love you. Cherish the time you spend with Me because I cherish it Myself. Life is hard and can harden your heart towards Me. Allow Me to bear your burden and life will become more bearable.

Stand upon My Word because it will stand forever. This life is a vapor and what you obtain will later be left behind. Give Me your worn out body and I will give you a life worth living.

A tough life was not meant for you to become toughened in life. My Son lived through the tough times because of His tender heart for Me. He loved Me. Love Me, too. I will show you what I can do for those who will continue to love Me, no matter what they go through.

September 12

Do not be afraid of living. You have been fearful in the past, but those things have now passed. You survived and still have more life to live.

Nothing can overtake you that you can't escape with My

love and direction. No force can overwhelm you because I AM greater than anything and anyone in this world.

Walk daily in truth and know that I AM working in you this very day. Peace is the environment you can live in when living for Me and Me living in you,.

Anything you face is only temporary, but My love for you lasts forever. Don't wait for tomorrow what you can experience today. Call on Me now. I want to hear you and give you My love and compassion.

September 13

Be glad you can enter My presence with thanksgiving. So many are unaware of My ever abiding presence they can know. Tell them of My love.

Tell them how they can know My Son, a loving Savior who died and rose again, so they too can live.

I AM with you always. But you don't always recognize and acknowledge Me. My Son came to tell you more about living and life. It is more than you are experiencing now. I AM with you forever, but life is also to be lived freely today.

Don't worry about tomorrow. We will walk together when tomorrow comes. Live today for Me and live it fully. I will bless you today if you trust Me in all your ways.

September 14

Doubts do arise, even during your strongest moments of faith. The enemy is never far away and that is why you need to stay close to Me. The enemy knows your weakest point, but I have always known it.

Allow Me to show you before he points it out to others. Don't be afraid of admitting your mistakes. I know them all.

Let others see you as a forgiven fellow traveler rather

than one who won't admit their wrongdoing. Honesty allows openness and an environment where I can do even greater works through you.

September 15

Find a reason to laugh today. You should be full of joy when you are full of My Spirit. My Son laughed, so why shouldn't you? You are not more holy by experiencing less laughter.

Live life with laughter. Smile at those who don't even know you. Say a cheerful word. Be more spontaneous and less calculating. Be like a child in My presence who knows I will take care of you. And I will.

September 16

You have been called and delivered. I set your path straight before you so you know where to go. I moved you along even though you felt mostly alone.

You have no sin too great that I can't forgive. You do nothing so wrong that changes My love for you. Rest in My peace and My presence. I AM with you to the journey's end.

Do not fear and do not be afraid. I have much for you to do for Me. I chose you to carry forth what I have given and spoken to you. Your heart has become tenderized over time. You hear Me and know Me. Others try to look and hear for a passing word.

I AM working in all things and making all things work for your best and My glory. You have been wounded and left to yourself. Others have not reached out to you, even after reaching out to them. You were left alone with no one really interested in what I was doing.

You now have something you had very little of in the

past. It is hope. You obeyed when you didn't know where it would lead. You were left for done, but I was always there. I AM still here.

September 17

The strength needed for today is now here for you. It is from Me at the time you need it most. The strength needed for tomorrow will be waiting on you. Slip it on as armor and, with faith, believe Me and My word.

Don't worry about the intensity of the storm and the violence of the wind whirling around you. They will cease the moment I give the command. The intensity makes no difference. It takes no additional effort on My part.

Meditate on the calmness. What you think about comes about. I AM here for you at this very moment. Don't try to figure out the future. Believe in Me for today and I will be there with you tomorrow.

I desire to be your in thoughts and peace will become present. Fall in love with Me again today and make Me the lover of your soul.

September 18

You have questions about the past, but it brought you here to the present. I AM working this very moment in your present circumstances. I AM forming them in order for you to be formed into the person I desire you to be.

Nothing happens without My knowledge. That is why everything can be used by Me. Therefore look for Me in every circumstance. I can bring honor to My name and honor to your name. Allow others to see My peace in you and feel My calmness all around you. Don't explain it. Just live it.

September 19

Someday you will better understand why you traveled this journey. It isn't yet over and I have more to show you and more to say to you.

Joy comes when you see the end results. I placed you on this path for the people who pass your way every day.

See it as a way to share My love to those who don't yet know how to fully trust Me. They are learners and need sharers who can tell them how to hear from Me and the importance of abiding in Me along the way.

Others were placed along your way to help you get where you are today. Reach out to others and allow them to know I AM there for them also.

September 20

The most important thing is to make Me most important today. You will see Me in a way that will bring hope tomorrow. Don't have any thoughts about what are in the days ahead.

You don't know and that is good. Because I know, that makes it better. I have the best for you in mind. Allow Me to bring it about by having no thoughts about tomorrow. I will take care of you.

Your provision will be there, just as I made it available for you yesterday. I brought it about and will do the same again. Why not trust Me? You have no one else who loves you more than Me.

September 21

Being set apart is done on your behalf to do My kingdom work on earth. The sacredness of My calling can be seen in your doing. Do what I assigned you to do in My name.

The life you live for Me does not end at the end of life's journey. What you do for Me on earth will be recognized in heaven. Those rewards will not be temporary, but will be for eternity.

Spend your time wisely. Invest in the lives of others and not in things that will be left behind for others to later possess. What is not eternal is of little value.

September 22

Harden not your heart because of the difficulties encountered in your life. They are here to tender your heart toward Me. I AM gentle in Spirit and fair in My judgments. That is why judgment is not to be made by others.

I look at the depth of one's soul and not just what is said and done. I know the reasons. I know the fears of one's heart.

The world cannot give you what I offer. I give you My peace. It is not in the world. It dwells within you. Allow it to rest on you as others come to recognize it is from Me.

You can't give it to them, but can tell them how it comes from Me. Make Me all that you have and I will give you all that you need.

September 23

Allow Me to love you in a way that you know it is Me. I AM the one who can extend love like you never experienced before. Becoming full of anxiety leaves little room for My peace. Worry makes the day seem long, yet it can shorten your life.

Allow Me to be on your mind at all times. I have things to say to you and you must be ready to hear My voice. Don't let the sounds of everyday living drown out My gentle whisper.

Stay focused and I will tell you what to do. I AM a part

of your entire life. Make Me that part and I will be with you wherever you go.

September 24

My beauty is all around you. Think of your life in the same way. You can see My creation in the rocks and hills, the valleys and mountaintops. I AM present when you see the bodies of water around you.

You will never be anywhere without seeing My creation. That is a reminder of who I AM and what I can do. Nothing you ask is beyond My power and I have no limits.

You only limit yourself when you limit your faith in Me. Believe for a miracle. Look for it. Acknowledge it came from Me and give Me the thanks.

September 25

You are a recipient of My love and blessings. They are in a storehouse to be showered upon you along this journey. Believe every day, even this very day, that you are special to Me with special blessings for you.

It doesn't have to be a special day because every day is special when you are My child. Love Me this very day as I show you My love for you. I have even more for you as you give daily more of yourself to me. I love to hear your words, "Here am I." As for Me, you know I AM always here.

September 26

I AM in the heavens, but I AM also inside of you. I dwell in the hearts of My children. I AM always with them and go wherever you go. I know of your pain and hurt. I also know of your joy and rejoice in your triumphs.

You will never go anywhere without Me. Neither will you ever be abandoned by Me. I AM with you until the end of the earth and beyond. Prepare yourself for the future by preparing your heart.

You prepare it by giving over all of yourself to Me. That includes your failures and your future. Mistakes don't move Me away from you. I AM as near today as I was on the day you felt the closest to Me.

Don't dread tomorrow. See it as a day where I will show you new things and a new way to experience Me.

September 27

Your future is not in the hands of another person. Not even your greatest enemy can pluck you from My hand. I cover you with My love and have a hedge around you. Nothing can touch you without My permission.

You live in a sinful world, but you don't have to partake of the sinful nature. I set you aside and set you apart from such a life.

My Spirit lives within you to guide you in all your ways. Don't look back with doubt. Look ahead with determination. Push ahead to the Promised Land where promises I made to you are waiting for you.

You don't have to walk this way again since I AM leading you to new heights every day. Rejoice in your victories as I restore the joy of your salvation. That is what you can make a joyful noise about.

September 28

Life is cluttered from things that are not from Me. It slows you down and often sends you down the wrong path. As you choose to move away from My leading, that will lead you into enemy territory. That is where danger lurks.

The enemy has nothing good for you and nothing good to say about you. Don't be fooled by the hollow promises and vain props the enemy uses to entice you into a trap. His way is not easy and neither is the burden light.

The enemy's trap is meant for evil. My way is meant for your good. I will neither harm you nor lead you astray. I AM the way and My way will lead you home.

September 29

You were wounded along the way, but I brought healing. You experienced pain, but I restored you. When you fell, I lifted you up. Everything I did for you was for your good.

I gave you friends to walk with you. I prepared you for the way you would travel. I anointed you with My oil of love and affection. My love for you may be questioned, but in time you will know.

Don't feel abandoned or forsaken. I never left you and you will never be without Me. Talk to Me, for I AM with you. Your words are heard by Me, even when no one is listening. You can hear more when silence is the most you hear. I will whisper of My love for you as you shout praises unto My name.

September 30

You doubted My ways. You questioned My moves. But I know where you are destined. It is a greater work for a greater cause. Your world is smaller, but I AM going to take you to greater heights. You cannot scale them without a special calling from Me.

The horizon is more than you can see. Your vision is limited, but My reach is beyond your comprehension. Don't try to limit My timelines. I AM not limited, but infinite. I cannot be contained in your world, but I can move you into a world beyond your world.

October 1

The stillness of the night and the silence of the soul are places I move and make Myself known. Many look for the masses who gather in My name. But sometimes the only thing they hear are sounds of their own making. I ask for just a simple joyful noise from you. That sound is music to Me.

I hear every sound uttered to Me. I interpret every language spoken and know the inner depths of your deep groaning. Make your needs known to Me and bring your petitions to Me. I desire to commune with you and reveal more of My love for you.

October 2

You can rest in Me because I AM in you. You can't tell Me what I don't know, but I ask you to bring your burdens to Me. You won't know what I can do until you give them to Me.

You were not built to bear such burdens. Remove them from your shoulders and place them upon Mine. I will make your load light if you worry less about your worries.

Worry doesn't add to your day but lessens its beauty. Allow My Spirit to break through the troubles that cloud your way. What you go through, I will see you through.

October 3

Give thanks in all things because all things can work together for your good and My glory. A confused mind cannot clearly hear My calling and My direction. Each day is a day traveled on the journey in life.

Make your move toward Me. Make this day count for Me. I do things in My name for your sake. I have your interest at heart and have a reason for every move I make upon your heart.

My presence may seem less present at times, but I AM always there. I will not leave you comfortless or abandoned. You can never escape My love. Neither can you outrun My presence.

I AM always with you. No step you make is without My permission. No direction you take will ever be hidden from My sight. Do all things for Me because I know all the things you do. Make the day about you and Me.

October 4

Don't focus on the road already traveled, but look ahead and see where I AM taking you. You can't see the destination from here, but you can see the daily progress toward it.

The more trust in Me makes the journey more peaceful. Turn a deaf ear to the daily noise and hear what I have to say in the silence of your soul. Remove yourself from the clamor and allow Me to calm your spirit and your soul.

Remove any doubt about what I AM doing. They slow down the release of My blessings and make the day less than fulfilling.

October 5

You desire to hear Me like others have in the past. I AM the same today as I was yesterday. Time makes no difference to Me. My word can be heard as clear today as yesterday.

Time does not mute My voice nor age My words. They are as meaningful to you as they were to others who struggled on their journey. They made it home and now you must make your way to that heavenly home.

My promises to you are not aged by time, but are as fresh as the morning dew. Be mindful of My presence and make all things about Me.

October 6

Your world is much bigger than what you see. There is more to do and be seen. I called you as My servant and you are to serve Me in a greater capacity.

There is a world of light in you that needs to be taken to those in darkness. With your light comes My truth. Speak kindly to those where I send you. Pray for those you see hurting. Share My love with those who need loving.

There are paths you will never journey again. Don't overlook the place I have you at a particular time. See what surrounds you and let others see Me in you. Some will see Me as how you see Me. Experience what I have now for you so others can experience that same intimate relationship.

October 7

Do not be afraid of what lies ahead. Have no fear of tomorrow. I have prepared the way for you and I AM waiting there for you. No enemy can overcome you if you put your trust in Me.

The enemy of this world has been overcome. He cannot overpower you without you allowing him to come over you. The enemy who dwells in darkness flees at My sight and words.

You have no reason to fear. Face tomorrow with confidence and watch those thoughts, that paralyze your mind, abandon their stronghold.

October 8

Someday you will see the reason for your past sorrow. It was used yesterday to take you where you need to be tomorrow. Before tomorrow arrives, today must be lived. It too will finally end, but not until I have you at the appointed place when the sun sets.

There is value left in today that must be mined. Continue to look for those nuggets of truth and diamonds of discovery that remain. Leave no blessing behind. Leave no truth unlearned. It is all for a reason and for your good.

October 9

See life the way I see it. There is beauty all around you. It is a reminder of My handiwork and My love of nature. The highest mountain and the deepest valley are signatures of what I see as beauty.

You are My creation and I see beauty in you. Your scars are rivers where mercy flows. Your pain reflects My deep work when you walked through the valley lows.

This conforms you into the image of My Son, which is the greatest expression of love ever known to earth. Let that beauty in you be a reflection of My love around you. Let them see it by letting them see what I do this day in you.

October 10

You waited for Me as I watched for this time. Your time has come for Me to show you the reason for such a time as this. You cried out to Me and no other during the dark nights of the soul.

You chose to wait on Me and not follow another path traveled by so many others. Now that you have waited, I choose this time to reveal My purpose for such a time as this.

October 11

Let your heart be purified with My presence. Allow nothing to stand between us as I draw you unto Myself. I created you to be at home in My presence. Hear My voice that called you the first time.

The world is hungering for My words and thirsting for My Spirit. Tell them how they can be filled. Speak kindness to them. Let mercy flow down like a river upon them. Make this day about Me and live your life accordingly.

October 12

Do not be afraid of things to come. I AM a God who intervenes in your life. I AM here to help you with your struggles and to lift your burdens. Let Me take your worries and cares upon Me. Those things cause you to lose sight of My presence in you.

Release each one to Me and stand tall with a new sense of hope and belief. Believe in Me and in My Word. Remember My promises. Read them out loud as a reminder to you about what I can do.

When it seems impossible, that is when all things are possible for those who abide in Me.

October 13

I never abandoned My children. Neither will I abandon you because you are My child. I will never neglect you nor leave you begging for bread. While others have no hope, you have hope in Me.

If you call upon Me, I will answer you. I will show you the way. And I will sustain you by giving you daily provisions.

October 14

You have come this far by faith. And your faith will take you home. Faith is what pleases Me. If you don't believe in what I AM able to do, you allow fear to replace faith.

Fear is an open door for the enemy. Faith is the door that leads to all possibilities. I will never let you out of My sight. Look for Me today. I will make Myself known for you to know I AM with you.

October 15

You see others who acknowledge My existence but don't fully allow Me to have full control of their lives. That comes through yielding to Me and knowing that I will guide your steps all along the way.

Your steps can take you toward Me or away from My will for your life. That plan is in place, but you must allow each day to be a step in that direction. Others will sense My presence in you when you allow Me to become your all.

October 16

You have nothing to say with a fresh anointing if you don't listen to My voice as I speak to your spirit. You must become still and listen. You can hear more if you step away from the noise of everyday living.

Cherish those moments alone with Me and open your spirit to My words. You were made to abide in a deep relationship with Me. How can you hear if you choose not to listen?

Time alone with Me is not time wasted. Each day is a new day and one not traveled before. Don't miss what I have to say to you. You are not the least of My children. I loved you from the beginning. Choose this day to be one lived for Me. By doing so, I give you new life for this new day before you.

October 17

The world cannot give you what I gave you. My Spirit and My words abide in you. Abide in My Word, the same words read by so many others.

Many did not experience that assurance because they chose not to believe. They hoped for things of this world which brought false hope and ultimately no hope.

Losing all hope means you have lost all faith. When you hope in Me, faith will direct you toward Me. I will place you on a sure foundation. That foundation is built upon My promise.

I will never let you down and will be waiting for you in your tomorrows. Live in My presence today. Know that I AM with you all the way.

October 18

You know I love you and that will never change. What changes is your love for Me. It ebbs and flows, based upon your circumstances. That will always change. Don't view my love in light of your circumstances.

See it in the light of the cross. I demonstrated it by giving you My Son to show you the way to Me. Follow the path that leads to the cross.

The resurrection of My Son can give you a resurrected life so you can experience My love for you today. Why should it change because of what you do? It's what He did that matters.

October 19

The world can't give you peace, but it can cause you not to experience it. Peace comes through trust, a relationship that will never be broken by Me. When you don't trust Me, you don't have the peace that only I can give.

Don't live a defeated life. Live it knowing that I AM with you and will be with you forever. My peace doesn't stop at death, but extends beyond. My Son gave it to you while on earth and will be with you in the hereafter.

It was not given just for later, but for this every moment. Listen to My voice. Feel My presence. Experience My peace. Life will be less painful when you experience more of My peace.

October 20

There is no one like Me, but there is also no one like you. There is more of a difference than you can perceive. I know why I made you and the reason for your existence. I aligned you for this time.

Your past has passed, but it brought you to this place. You may not yet know, but soon it will be fully known by you and by some others. There are others who will never believe this was Me working in you during this entire time.

I don't begin a work and then walk away. My hand is upon you the whole time. If I remove it, the enemy will try to remove you from this earth. But you will not leave until I pronounce it.

Others may judge you, but withhold your own judgment until the sun sets on your life for the final time.

October 21

Believe in Me, for I believe in you. If you know I work in your life, why would I stop before your life ends? There is purpose in the plans I created for you. You are not a mistake and you have not been misplaced.

You must look for Me in order to see Me. Read My promises in My Word. They do not fade away or won't be finalized until I have the final word.

Your mind cannot comprehend the depth of every detail in your life. There are no surprises for Me since I see everything from the beginning to the end. You think of your life as a dot on the line of eternity.

That dot was placed at this point in time. Live it fully and purposefully. Your time will end and there will be no more time to make a difference for Me.

October 22

Make your way to the Promised Land. There will be a bounty of blessings that will bring you delight and abounding joy. Joshua and Caleb tasted of the spoils before others entered Canaan.

I have blessings for you now so you can taste of what is ahead for My children. Allow Me to bless you now so you will know what will be there for others. Tell them of My goodness and mercy. Taste and see. There is so much more, for I AM much more than you can know.

October 23

You, My child, have experienced a long journey, even though you still have some travel time left on earth. You know your destination, but didn't know the route you would take.

It was My doing that took you this way. Any other way would not bring you to where you are today. The purpose is for you to experience the goodness of My love for you.

See what I AM doing. I began this work early in your life in order to experience the harvest days you are now entering. Be blessed and know these days of rejoicing are for you and are from Me.

October 24

I AM revealing to you the impact your life for Me has made on others. You can't see in the spiritual realm what I see of you in others. Words that were earlier spoken and deeds done in My name have brought forth fruit in others' lives.

Never underestimate how you were used by Me when you thought you were making very little difference in the life you lived in front of them.

You will see the results of your labor, but not all will be revealed. It will be after your life when you will see what I did through you. It's not so much about the big things, but the consistent things that made a difference.

October 25

Continue to come into My presence. Seek My face and My will for you. Life is in constant motion and you need to hear what I say to you. Being still is different than standing still. You can't remain where you are spiritually if you are to continue the spiritual journey.

Take the time to be still and know Me. Then move along and make Me known to others.

Commotion does not invite communion. Be deliberate in listening and learning more about Me. Today's bread will become stale tomorrow. Yesterday's time with Me will not always be sufficient for future days.

Know Me and learn more about Me daily. More revelation will be needed as you move throughout life. Less revelation means more difficulty for you.

October 26

I remember the days you wept when you felt so disjointed. You knew Me, but really didn't know much about Me. Learning more is a result of living more. Each situation reveals more of who you are and more of who I AM and can be to you.

I revealed what you needed to know then. I AM revealing more of Myself to you now, even though it remains partially hidden. More is to come. Accept what you know for this day. Look for Me and you will see more of Me.

Wrap yourself in My peace for this part of your journey. It will take you through any storm that is blowing across the sea of uncertainty.

Calmness in Me brings about calmness in your circumstances. Clouds will dissipate and you will see how I saw you through.

October 27

You wonder if others have doubts just as you. Some more. Some less. You are responsible for the way you believe in Me. Trust Me for what you know. And trust Me when you don't know. All is known to Me, even when you don't know what to believe anymore.

Doubts only create confusion. Trust creates peace. You can't see what I see. You don't know the obstacles or the best road to travel. I will lead you to the path of righteousness and restoration.

See now what I will do, even though you may not understand why. Leave that to Me.

October 28

There are many variations in life. You have your highs and your lows. The lows can go to some of the lowest points in your life. Your depths of despair don't affect Me. I will be with you when all is dark and you are grasping for survival.

I desire to see you demonstrate your faith and not be as if I never rescued you before. I was there then. And I AM with you now. You have My peace and My protection. It's a process you experience when you go through the fire.

Sense My presence and see Me work. These times prepare you for those times ahead. You will know I AM with you. Recognize My trust and value it. It is needed because of the uncertainty that is unfolding in the world today. These can be great times of victory as you build your trust in Me.

October 29

My peace can always be with you, regardless of your circumstances. As the wind signals an upcoming storm, you can know for certain I AM there with you.

Storms will draw you closer to me as you seek shelter, or it can drive you away as the rain of discouragement causes a downpour on your faith.

Think of the storms as a time to feel My presence and give you an inner calmness. Hope in Me will keep you buoyed in the rough seas. Nothing can overcome you that I can't stop. There is no need to fear the enemy because the enemy fears Me and runs from My presence.

October 30

Don't dwell on your mistakes. That is where the enemy wants your focus. He tries to set you up for failure when he reminds you of the times you failed. Why do you forget so quickly what I have done for you so recently?

I will be there for you and help you through. I AM the same God of ancient times. Their faith wavered at times, but persevered in the hardest of times. You can experience so much now if you allow Me to be to you the kind of God I desire to be.

You only know fragments of My existence. Let Me show you the great and mighty things you can do in My name. Transform your thinking and I can transform your world.

October 31

The sun brings warmth as it encompasses your entire being. Allow Me to love you in a way where you will sense Me all around you. When light dissipates and darkness moves in, it doesn't mean I AM moving out. It is fear that comes over your thinking and overcomes you.

Exercise your faith and I will exercise My power over your most deep seated fear. Don't become paralyzed with doubt. Just believe. Really believe in My power and see the darkness shattered by My light.

Darkness does not always remain on earth. It gives way to light. Put your faith in Me this day and you will not be in total darkness. I AM that light for you to make it through this present day of darkness.

November 1

Think of My Spirit when you think of My Son. My Son came and returned. I sent the Holy Spirit and He remains.

My Spirit was not given to you as an afterthought. My Son told you He needed to leave so My Spirit would be imparted.

My Spirit is not an option for everyday living. He is needed, but you seldom realize He is an extension of Me on earth, just as Jesus lived among you.

Let My Spirit be the stabilizing factor in your life. He was there when I created you and now He is in you. Why do you not call upon Him to intercede for you? The Spirit is your force placed in you when My Son came into your life.

The enemy wants you to remain in darkness about the potential power that is in you. Call upon Me and watch My Spirit become unleashed in you. That is the greatest fear of the enemy because he knows of its greatest potential. Use what is in you. That is why My Spirit is in you.

November 2

My joy is to see you experience happiness along the way. Life is difficult, but can be lived with expectancy and joy. I created the beauty of the earth. I created you to have relationships with others. I also desire you to experience the joy of your salvation.

Hold on to My promises and the truth about My purpose for your existence. You cannot know if you do not go the way I have planned. I AM sovereign, but I also give you the choices on certain decisions.

Make them wisely with a sound mind. Be at peace and be mindful of My peace that comes with My presence.

November 3

Some day you will see the life you lived from the way I see it. You can only see the present. Soon you will come to the knowledge of a better understanding how I caused all things to work for My good and your good.

My reason comes first. Your understanding will come later. See to it that no doubts or fears dismay you. They will only serve as roadblocks that cause you to not experience the uniqueness of your journey. Be open to My ways and listen to My voice. I will tell you the way.

November 4

Make time in your schedule for Me. I AM the most important being in your life and I can affect every move and thought that comes to you this day. Believe what you believed in the past before your way became clouded with doubts and your mind filled with anxiety.

I have an even greater day planned for you if you believe My Word and experience My strength. It's not about barely making it in life. So much of My blessings have been left behind when they were available for your asking and believing.

See the day as one I make Myself known. Know that My way is the best way that is filled with better days ahead. My plans are specific.

My calling calls for you to travel a less traveled road and has more for you than you could ever give thanks. Believe and see. Believe with the mind and see it come about beginning now.

November 5

Your journey is different because I set you on a path that seems very narrow and winding. It is an unusual path because your life was not to be in the mainstream. I showed you things along the way through your dark valleys and turbulent storms.

You thought you were beaten down, but it made you even stronger. It caused you to rely on My strength and made you lean on Me when no one else listened to your cries of anguish and sorrow.

Life is not over and your journey has yet to be completed. In time it will end. But until then, I will show you joy unspeakable. You can now experience Me in a way you thought would never come about.

You will now begin to see more sunlight along the way. You will now feel My warmth as I smile because you never gave up, even when you seemingly had no hope. No more worries about tomorrow, only joyful anticipation of the upcoming blessings.

November 6

Those who feel forsaken have not been forgotten. I keep them in the palm of My hand for safekeeping, even when they feel I no longer intervene in their world.

You see what I AM doing in your life. You are set apart and sanctified. You now see why you took this questionable journey. You had questions, but I had the answers. I knew what I was doing all along, even when you couldn't see your way through.

Where you were was not a mistake. Where you are now is where I have you for now. You must still have endurance because of what you have endured so far.

Instead, think about the rewards that are waiting for you. Blessings upon blessings will bring forth sounds of joy from your lips and praise for Me.

November 7

When I gave you My Spirit, I gave you My power. It is your resource as you journey on this road of life. It is not to be buried in your mind or never used. My Son used this same power manifested in Him through My Spirit in Him.

Believe My words and believe in the power within you. You can speak to the mountain in your life. My power is greater than any force on earth or in the heavens.

The enemy trembles at My name, but runs from My power. Command the forces of evil to flee in My name. Unleash My power by speaking My commands in My Word. Fear your enemies no more, but put fear in them by moving in My power.

November 8

You thought you saw the good years of your life passing by. There are still good years remaining and more that you are to do for My kingdom. You will not know the impact of your walk with Me that was made on the hearts and minds of others until you are by My side. Then I will tell you the whole story.

Don't measure your life by where you are and what you have. My Son lived a simple life. He had nowhere to lay His head that He could call His own.

You see others who measure success by the size and the cost of a home. It will be left behind and someone else will buy it, measuring their success by the same home.

Life is to be lived with your residency in heaven on your mind at all times. Store up blessings by doing My work on earth. Share My love. Tell others of My salvation for them and how to live abundantly while living here in this temporary home called earth.

November 9

Be at peace from all the rules and mandates of man that tell you how you have to live for Me. I only need your faith and trust. Those two will guide you to Me and I will set you free from the entanglements of religiosity.

Rules bind your spirit and don't allow the freedom you have in Me. Those who restricted others by trying to enforce their commands were called hypocrites.

I did not call them to be enforcers of the law. Instead, you are to be an encourager and set others free from such bondage. Be free in Me and not in bondage to those whose beliefs only serve as restrictions.

November 10

No one knows of all your struggles but Me. I AM the only one that needs to know. Most of your friends don't need to know. They will only move to the other side of the road as they pass you by. Some will think your dilemma is what you did to bring it upon yourself.

I see where you are and hear your cries from My vantage point. Others are unable to see that way and cause them to have a misaligned picture. They will only say, "Be blessed," and move on their way.

My plan for you is still in place. It even brought you to this place. The valley must be encountered before you can move up the mountain that ascends into My presence and My blessings.

Don't look back yet because you will not come to the full realization of My calling upon your life until a little farther on the journey. Your steps are still being ordered by Me.

November 11

You have not seen what I AM about to do in your life and in your world. No one knows the foundation I laid at the beginning to bring about such a completion for this time in your life.

You don't see the foundation that is below ground level. Nor do others see what is below the surface of your life. They will soon see the finished product and come to the realization the vastness of My calling and My work in you.

A building is not built in one day. Neither is the work in your life. At some point, I will say, "It is finished." Then is when you can see the results of your labor and the beauty of My work in you from the very beginning.

November 12

You do not walk alone. I AM beside you all the way. Others may desert you. Friends may go away during the night, but I will never leave you.

Don't go on feelings, but move in faith. That is your guiding light that will put you on the right road during this stretch of your journey. Be not afraid, for I AM with you.

Darkness is seen as light to Me. Nothing is hidden. The enemy cannot hide, but will flee from My presence.

You have My favor. You know My voice. Move into the Land of Promise that was promised to you from the beginning. You are loved by Me, dearly loved and the desire of My heart. Be at peace and see My work all around you.

November 13

When darkness comes to others, you will be the light that beckons them to Me. Do not be afraid of the dark, for that is where you will see My work take place and My grace abound.

See to it that no one tells you any differently. You are Mine and Mine alone. Today My peace will overwhelm you. I will come to you as the morning sun overcomes a land of darkness.

Be a light and show others the light. They will see all that I AM doing in you and through you. My presence will be welcomed when you see My work and My favor in you. Be at peace and enjoy this day that was made by Me for you.

November 14

You are called with a holy calling and to have a presence of holiness about you. It gives hope to others when they see peace around you and purpose for you.

A calling brings about a confirmation. The confirmation causes a realization that you are indeed set apart. You live among the masses, yet you are different. That causes others to see you as peculiar.

My people are peculiar when My presence dwells in their midst. You cannot stay where you are today. You must take another step in the future. Don't be left behind. There is more for you today and even more to experience tomorrow.

November 15

You feel your life has been mostly one of subtraction. Much has been extracted from you, even those things you counted as blessings. You wonder why a God of much has taken much away from you.

What I removed is to make room for what I AM about to replace. Old wineskin is unable to hold the new wine. That is why I had to do a new work in you.

What I now give you cannot be spilled out onto the ground and can't be reproduced. My kingdom is about added blessings and multiplying the number of people you will touch.

You have a new mind that can now comprehend the things from Me. Before now, you could only see from a distance what I was doing with My kingdom on earth. No longer are you to see it from afar.

I AM working up close and personal in you. Do not be afraid of the future. Shout praises as you enter into a new realm.

Never before have you seen what I AM revealing this very day. Be sensitive and be looking for a new work at a different level in the spiritual realm.

November 16

Your tears soaked the pillow when I seemed to be so distant. That caused you to doubt the days of closeness. Those days were really Me. But that is not all of Me. There is more ahead because there is more of Me that is being made known.

Seek Me first and everything else becomes secondary. Don't allow the enemy to plunder the promises I made earlier to you. They are now coming to pass.

Today is a new beginning in this journey. The day ends with a sunset and begins as the sun rises again. Beginning a new day doesn't mean you are beginning a new journey. It's a continuation, but with new revelation. I reveal more along the way. Learn every day and look forward to each new day.

November 17

Why do you forget so quickly the assurance I gave you that I AM with you and will be your Guide? The way is uncertain for you, but I know the way for you to go. It will take you into a new realm of My understanding and you were called to travel this journey.

You are not here by mistake. Neither are you at a dead end. Although you can't see what is in front of you, you must trust Me. I assured you and revealed Myself along the way.

You would not have seen Me if I wasn't there with you.

Be at peace and experience calmness in your soul. Anxiety has no place in the heart of a believer who truly trusts Me. Show more trust and I will show you more of the way.

November 18

Part of spiritual living is growing. Ask yourself each day what can you learn from Me. A soldier needs more than basic training. Additional skills and behaviors are part of the growth process.

Practice what you have already been taught. You must be more advanced to advance more of My kingdom's work on earth.

David became skilled while alone. Use the lonely times to prepare through prayer and allowing My Word to soak into your mind. Be filled with My Spirit. Bring light into darkness. Bring joy to the hearts of others.

November 19

Don't look at life with its limitations. Look beyond the now. See what I AM doing to prepare you for the conquering days ahead. Deception can cause a detour, even for a moment.

Believe the Truth, who is My Son. Believe My Word, which was God-breathed. A delay will only cause you not to enjoy the benefits earlier.

You have crossed the most rugged part of the mountains. There are only a few hills and small valleys left to travel. It will be easier because of how much you have gone through.

You knew somewhere along the way that it had to get better, even though you never became bitter. Is the best yet to come? It is yet to come and will come soon, very soon.

November 20

Trust Me for your future needs. You worried about the future. Much of that future has already passed. As you passed through it, I was there with you. Your needs were met. You still have needs and I will still be there.

My supply is endless. No matter how much was given out, the supply remains the same. Make the next step one that causes you to step into the future. Hesitancy will only hinder the process.

Delayed faith brings about a delay in your needs being met. Be firm in your faith and I will give you a firm foundation that cannot be cracked or swept away.

November 21

You were created for this day, but this day was also created for you. It's not about the day, but what is done in My name during the day. As the light breaks forth that indicates a new day, the light of My love in you is to be shown all around you.

Don't think of the difficulties you could encounter today. Many of them will never make it to the surface. Don't dwell on what has not yet happened, but think about the good things that are about to take place.

Today you will encounter an unknown joy you didn't know was coming your way. Let Me take care of your concerns. Make this day count by showing your love to Me and sharing My love with others.

Have no fear of the unknown the day holds. I will be with you and hold your hand. The more you sense My presence, the more peace you will have within.

November 22

You know My heart for you because I have shown it in so many ways. I drew you close to Me at times when you thought you were alone. Never once did I leave you unprotected. You were kept safely under My loving care.

The way to experience more life is to give more of yourself and My love to others. Life goes beyond your world. It's also about invading the lives of others and sharing My love which can pierce the darkness of their souls.

The more light you give, the more you will receive. Don't hide your light under a canopy or block it out with wrongdoing. Be aware of the check I put in your spirit to keep you holy.

A pure vessel brings forth the purest light. The light is not only to be bright, but also to be pure.

November 23

I AM your refuge. Take comfort in Me as the storm passes through your life. The darkness is only for the moment, but My love for you is forever. Calmness will soon follow and you will see how I providentially protected you.

You shall soon see why it was important to experience your past turmoil. You not only have a hiding place in Me, but also a higher place to experience Me.

Life is more than keeping the Laws. It's also about giving to others what I have entrusted to you. Your gifting is unique. Your work on earth is not yet complete. Don't live in fear of tomorrow. Be at peace and know of My work in you.

You didn't arrive randomly at the place you are today. You are here for such a time as this. See what I AM doing by seeing how I AM using you to bless others around you. Be still now and know that I AM God.

November 24

The kingdom of God belongs to those where My kingdom rules in their hearts. That is where I AM the God of their universe and life revolves around My being.

I AM with you, but you must allow yourself to be all about Me. The more you give to Me, the more I can make of you. I want you to experience all that life has to offer in its original state.

Man has fallen and I want to lift you up. Most believers have become satisfied with the status quo and chose to live according to their standards. Make life all about Me. Make it count for Me and then you will be unable to count all My blessings coming your way.

November 25

Your life is to be lived for Me. I have so many blessings that wait for you. Yet you still look for scraps on earth that you think will satisfy your present hunger.

Scraps are like husks to the prodigal son. They fill your belly, but don't fill your hunger for the kingdom. Serve Me where you are today.

Tomorrow I move you to another place that will allow your light to shine even brighter. You don't have to work at it. Just live it.

November 26

You went through a period where you questioned My existence. Your spiritual mind seemed cut off from Me and heard nothing. You didn't see Me moving in your life, but I was moving in your world around you.

The shut down time brought on silence. I was doing a

reconstruction in your life to be better prepared for tomorrow. Today is the entrance point for the future.

Your future begins now. You are in it, so live it for Me. Talk no longer about what life will be like, but about how you see Me in your current circumstances.

You thought what you went through was bad, but it all worked out for the good. See what I have done for you and how I AM making all things work out best for you, which is good.

November 27

Your sins have been washed away. The night is now turning into day. It allows you to see life as you have never seen it before. See what I AM doing because of what I have already done.

Sense My presence and feel the peace I bring to you. Do not let your heart be troubled. Believe that I will complete the good work I began in you. Life is made for you to live it with Me.

Have no regret about past experiences. I can turn downfalls into testimonies. Share with others how you stumbled and now have been lifted up to a higher plane of life with Me.

I bring you up and don't put you down. Your enemy has nothing good to say about you. Don't repeat his lies. Remember My promises and believe on Me. See Me with open arms and an open heart of love and forgiveness.

November 28

One day you will see you had this calling along with this cross in your life. My Son was called and He had a cross to carry. Blessings come by humbling yourself before Me.

My blessings should also bring you into a sense of humility, knowing none of this is possible outside of Me.

Many followers will see very little of a rewarding life in a lifetime. Recognition usually comes when you are no longer here to hear praise from others. What lasts eternally will be seen in the end.

Don't listen for praise from others, but rather look how you can share My love with them. Life is about giving. Give to others so you can receive more from Me.

November 29

Friendships are a part of life, but you will never have a friend as My Son, Jesus. He paid the ultimate price when you never knew Him. But I had you in mind when He became your Deliverer and Savior.

The more you come to know Him, the more you will sense a heart full of love from Me. He came to you as the only way to Me. There is no other way. My Son's tomb is empty and His return to Me validates My love for you.

There is no other way and those who receive Me are the ones I will receive unto Myself.

November 30

Pray for others as you would have them pray for you. Not everyone prays when they tell you they are praying. But you are to pray for those whom I tell you to pray. Warfare is done in the heavens and is manifested on earth.

Prayer does change things. I can change your circumstances, relationships, your future, and My intimacy with you. I long for the time you spend alone with Me. That is also a way I direct you how to pray for others.

Say very little about your prayers. That is your lifeline to Me and not a way to be recognized by others. More manipulated recognition here will mean less reward in heaven.

I know your heart. I also know of your love for Me. Live each day as an opportunity to bless others. That is also how you are a blessing and have a reward.

December 1

The morning dawns when the sun breaks through the morning mist. Light shows what is all around you that you never saw in the dark. As you walk in My light, you see how I ordered your steps and the way I moved you away from the traps and pitfalls along the way. The enemy meant it for destruction. I meant it for a dependence upon Me.

No one has a love for you like My love. I desire a love in return when all your trust is in Me. Trust provides the peace and manifestation of My presence. I must be seen by you in order for others to see Me in You.

Peace is what you desire. You can't explain it until you experience it. It can be a continuous presence if you will be sensitive to the Holy Spirit. He is a being, and a part of Me and My Son. Make the best of this moment and rest in My arms of love.

December 2

You knew the way and entered into it. I now show you the path to travel and journey to take. I now lead you into paths of righteousness near the streams of My mercy. There is where you will find Me.

When you encounter Me, you will experience My peace that I have specifically for you. I satisfy your longing. That is what you want from Me and I now give you. Life is not about what it used to be, but what it can be.

You are My instrument of praise and you are being played

to bring a sweet, sweet sound to My ear.

December 3

I AM here with you. You will never be outside of My presence because of My love that surrounds you. Be at peace and do not fret over things out of your control. It simply means I can do all things and can bring everything under My control.

Do not let other people's lack of concern about their inconsistent walk be a concern to you. They have the light but choose not to walk in it on a consistent basis. Love them but don't let them lead you astray. You know the way to Me, so walk in it.

December 4

You know of My presence because you have drawn near to me. There is more, much more I have for you. You see a glimpse of it, but haven't walked in the full glory of it.

I didn't call you only to make you struggle. Following Me does call for a life of sacrifice, but not one of struggling. I do allow testing.

My supply is more than abundant. It is overflowing for those who exercise simple, but solid faith in Me. Be steadfast in your relationship with Me. Be that solid rock that shall not be moved. Be that lighthouse that directs others to Me.

You live a different life because I made you differently and set you on a different path than other family members and friends. They see you as a question mark, but I will put the exclamation point when your life makes its final statement.

December 5

Draw near to Me and I will draw near to you. I never left you or turned away from you. A moment of doubt will not break our relationship. It causes you to sense some added distance between us. It is you that moved away from Me.

My love for you is unchanging. I cannot love you more and I will not love you less. Pursue Me and experience more of Me than ever before. There is so much more, yea even much, much more.

December 6

Be confident and be at peace. One causes the other to be experienced. I AM your Savior in the storm. Experience My peace inside you when your world on the outside is in turmoil.

You are one of My favored ones. Others see you on the outside, but what I do is on the inside. You have rest coming your way. Restlessness causes you to rest less. Rest is what you desire and that is My want for you.

There is too much beauty in living for Me that you are missing. See the good in all people. See Me at work in all places. I AM all that you need and will see you to the end.

December 7

There are others waiting for you in heaven who want to see you finish your race well. Some really knew your heart. Others didn't understand you. But when the big picture is seen, they will know you were headed the right way all along.

No one is to be your judge, but My Son. He will judge fairly and faithfully because of His walk on earth. He will judge with purity in His heart and holiness in His mind. He knows of My plans for you and your heart in the pursuit of that plan.

Today My presence will be made known and you will know it is Me. Believe in Me. Believe that all things are possible I send your way and have for you. See to it that you trust Me for everything and in all things.

December 8

Make time for Me. Do not let the things of the world take the time you can spend with Me. Calm your soul. Let your spirit be at rest. Restlessness is to stay on the outside. Don't take in what is to be left out.

Thinking the wrong thoughts was the downfall of My first created beings. Think of My goodness and see how I change things for your good. See how much I love you when you give more of yourself over to Me.

If you want more of Me, then give Me more of you. My love for you is unsurpassed by anything on earth or in heaven. Open your arms and your heart for Me. Fill every area of your life with My love. Know Me as never before. Allow Me to love you as you have never been loved by anyone before.

Mine is unconditional. I don't have any conditions that need to be met. Meet Me today with a mind bent for Me.

December 9

Faithfulness is what pleases Me. Your faith followed you through the storms. Hope was almost lost, but your faithfulness saw you through. Testing has now turned into triumph.

The sky is clearing because of the light of understanding. You see now the reason for your journey. It was not hopeless and you never gave up. My love for you gives you hope and causes you to live another day for Me.

I AM not far away, but dwell in your midst. Feel My love

and sense My presence. Nothing else matters. Your love for Me is to be foremost in your life. Fall in love with Me and be overwhelmed by My compassion.

I make right what was wrong. Those who wronged you will know My vengeance. Vindication for you will be Mine, all Mine.

I delight in bringing low those who opposed Me and defied My existence. Their words condemn them. They take pleasure in scoffing, but will soon be silenced.

December 10

Even on good days you see some doubts linger. You only know what your mind comprehends and what you experience for the moment. Your world is only as big as your comprehension.

My power is unlimited. I can create with a word or set things into motion with a thought. Become more aware by allowing My thoughts to override your thoughts. What happens does not come from randomness.

Your life is measured by days. I know from beginning to end. I created you to experience Me while on earth. I AM infinite, but there is no distance between us. My Spirit lives in you to guide you daily how to live for Me.

December 11

Your thoughts cost you blessings. You have not because you do not ask in faith and believe. You see Me as a God only as big as your imagination.

Train your thoughts to see Me as an all sufficient God whose supply never diminishes. Begin by rejoicing in Me. That will lead to a different end. You will see what you would have missed if you had not changed the way you view Me. Thank Me for what has been given you.

Praise Me for what you are about to gain. A change now will bring about a different direction and a new relationship. Try Me and I will show you great and mighty things.

December 12

You dreamed of life better than what you experienced in the past. For the moment you still have hope that something will change. You can't control your circumstances but I can change your heart.

Give it to Me once again and see the change I bring about. It is up to you if you give your all to Me. The more of yourself you allow Me to control, more of your life will come under My control.

I AM the God of the good times and I AM also with you in the valley. I will always be wherever you are and I can take you where you need to be. Look for Me in all the situations that you are placed.

Sense My presence and listen for My directions. I will not deceive you, but will keep you protected. You have nothing to fear. I can intervene at any moment. I can send angels that will block any intrusion of the enemy.

See in your mind the enemies scattering as I break strongholds in your mind. Your mind is Mine when you keep your thoughts on Me.

December 13

You see others live their lives with little thought about Me. They want control of life and their destiny. Soon they will have no control and will cry desperately out for Me. That is when many will question My existence because I did not intercede.

I AM not a stop gap God that only allows Me to have access for their wants. They will call but I will not answer.

I hear those who call for Me to be their God in all things. I AM a just God, but I AM also a jealous God. I want to be in your life in everyday living and not just at those times of rescue.

Keep Me in your mind. Keep Me in the center of your thoughts. That's when you can see Me in all things at all times.

December 14

One cannot predict life, but you can complicate it by questioning what life is about. You were created to abide in Me. Abiding takes the concerns of the future and places them before Me.

I take those concerns and exchange them for My peace. If you don't have peace, then you still claim those concerns as your responsibility. You must go through certain situations as a refiner's fire where purity is instilled and things not of Me are removed. I know what is to be removed.

You cling to worry and concerns as if they are your means of survival. They are obstacles set in your path by the enemy. I can remove a mountain as easily as a pebble. Believe and it shall be done.

December 15

You wonder what is the best way to experience life. Life is not just about the present, but also about life eternally. You think about your present situation as if it will always be with you. The present will soon become the past and can only be reflected upon.

Don't enter the future with an empty present. I have more for you, but you must be engaged in living for Me daily. Be living for Me fully in order for Me to give you a life fully alive.

I AM the great I AM and there is nothing that can over-ride My power. Draw unto Me and you will see more of life from My perspective, even the reason why you are passing this way in life.

December 16

The words I gave to you in the past will not return void and empty. What I declare is backed up with My power. Nothing I declare can be overturned by the enemy of dark-ness.

His power was broken at Calvary. He can only influence your thoughts and tempt you. Your actions are a result of the decisions you make with your thoughts. The enemy's power can be shattered by a single word spoken by Me.

You have the power to remove the enemy from any pres-ent stronghold in your life. "Say to this mountain." You speak to those areas of your thoughts and actions that are blocking the blessings I have for you. They are on the other side.

Your words and your belief in what I can do are the keys to unleash a ravaging attack upon those who wage the war in your mind. There is no need to walk in darkness when I AM the light of your world.

December 17

You listened for My voice as one who was alone in the wilderness. How could you hear My voice if I was not with you? You heard because I spoke. You sensed My nearness because I was near.

You are not alone and neither are you without direction. I have your steps in order because there were ordained from the beginning. It doesn't matter about the smallness when you began your journey with Me. It is about the fullness of the calling.

Finish the journey in My fellowship and limitless love. Experience what you have longed for by seeing Me in every move you make. I AM there and will see you to your journey's end.

December 18

I speak to you through circumstances, but I AM much bigger than what you see happening to you and all around you. I can use anything and all things to conform you into the follower that pleases Me.

Nothing happens outside of My control. There is nothing I cannot use to bring about My purpose.

One day there will be peace on earth, but you now can have peace in your heart. I give it and only you can receive it for yourself. You accepted Me in your life. Now accept all the love I give you.

December 19

Don't dwell on your present difficulties. Meditate on My goodness. Tomorrow will begin a change. Worrying about the future has no future. Your future is the present. You do not know what tomorrow may bring, or even if you have a tomorrow.

Not living for today will bring about regrets tomorrow. You have My promises. Remind yourself that My word for you is as good today as it was when I gave it to you.

Your circumstances may not be shaping up to your anticipation. The day is not over. I can bring about a complete turnaround by causing even a single event to change.

If you trust Me, then trust My word that is in My Word as well as My words that enter your spirit.

December 20

You are a delight, especially when you trust in Me. There is no obstacle too large to overcome that can stand in the way between you and Me. Mountains are not always barriers, but to help you be able to see what I AM doing in your life and to see My beauty all around you.

Lonely times can be lovely times with Me. Solitude makes a good environment for Me to speak to your thoughts. That is when I can share what needs to be heard. The noise all around you can drown out what I have to say.

Be still and know that I AM God. I AM the same God that I was to Abraham, Isaac, and Jacob. Those accounts are not folklore, but recorded events that took place on earth during the time of their lives.

Listen to My voice and look for Me. But sometimes you must stop and be still before you can go on any farther with life.

December 21

Tears formed in your eyes when you laid your head on the pillow. But I formed all of you and know all about you. My angels see you during those lonely times, so you are not alone.

Rise up from your bed of sorrow and follow Me. I prepared a place for you here on earth before you occupy a place in heaven.

I AM with you now. I not only see your dilemma, but also have My angels there to watch over you and see you through to the end of your journey. You are not alone, but you do need to spend some time alone with Me.

There are things you need to know. You may not know all, but I can tell you enough to let you know I AM with you. Fear nothing and faith everything. Know that I AM with you in all things and I can be all things to you during that time.

December 22

No one knows you better than Me, so why do you look for the favor of others? They don't know you like I do and can't make a sound judgment about where you are in relation to Me.

They may not understand what I tell you. They don't hear what I speak to your spirit. Don't ask for their opinions and don't look for their favor. I will vindicate you at My proper time.

I know when to reveal what I have been doing in your life. Others will know it was Me all the time because I did make Myself known to you.

Do not give up or give in. I have more for you to see and more that I will make known. When you see, there will be no doubt that it was Me.

December 23

I will resurrect the work you did in My name that others may see. They saw what you did, but chose not to see what I was doing in you. What you did was not fully recognized because they didn't see Me doing a work in you at that time.

Some are too busy trying to do things in My name and fail to recognize how I AM speaking to them through what I AM doing in you.

They fail to see how I can work through others when they are too busy trying to let others see how I AM working in themselves.

It's not about who can do the most for Me, but who chooses to be the servant and humble themselves before Me. The least in the kingdom are the greatest. They know they are nothing and can't do anything outside of Me. Make yourself the least and that is when I can do the most.

December 24

You must move with Me in order to see more of Me. You cannot live off yesterday's manna. I AM doing a new work and want to take you to a new level in Me. There is more to know than what you previously learned.

You can do no more if you choose not to follow Me anymore. The wilderness is not the place to die when I have a better place for you to live. The deserts and the valleys in life are places to pass through, not to die there.

There is the other side, but there is still another side I have for you. You are not to stay in the realm you currently occupy. There is more, but you must choose once again to move forward in My name. That's how you get closer to the other side.

December 25

See how others thirst for Me. I AM the living water that flows through you. My presence is to be made known through you that can provide hope to others. You must not keep Me inside of you.

Release what I placed in you and then is when you can receive even more. A fresh daily supply of who I AM is ready to occupy you. Give to others so I can give you more.

More of Me is what you want. I can give you more if you give more of yourself to others. My Spirit comes in so it can go out to others. My supply is unlimited and you will never run dry.

December 26

Deep inside your being is a big God. It is Me who wants to do a bigger work than ever before. You know it is there, but you can't seem to bring it to life. I AM the one who established it within you and can make it your life. That life will be about Me.

You have a past life and a future in your life. You can't live in either one for the moment. You must live in the present. That is where your currently live. Move your thinking away from the past. Know you have a future, but realize this moment is to be about Me.

Seek first My kingdom and then these others things will be taken care of in the future. Don't lose this moment, but seize it. Shore up your belief in Me. Have a strong faith that can withstand the storms that try to blow you off course.

Keep Me in your sight and My Word in your heart. Hold to My promises and see Me in all your surroundings. Seek Me. Go on a God hunt and there you will find Me wherever you go.

December 27

You listened for My voice as one who was alone in the wilderness. How could you hear My voice if I was not with you? You heard it because I spoke. You sensed My nearness because I was near.

You are not alone and neither are you without direction. I have your steps in order because they were ordained from the beginning.

It doesn't matter of the smallness when you began your journey with Me. It is about the fullness of the calling. Finish the journey in My fellowship and limitless love. Experience what you have longed for by seeing Me in every move you make. I AM there and will see you to your journey's end.

December 28

Your quiet time can be quite a time with Me that can cause your sorrow to see the light of My love once again. When I AM near, don't be distracted by anything around you. I have something to say to you.

I AM your Maker. Allow Me to make you in a way that I AM the One that can be seen. You won't have to tell if others can see for themselves.

Be the one that dares to be different. Allow Me to take your burdens from you and you wear the crown of righteousness and right standing because of the work I continue to do in your everyday living.

December 29

The mountains won't be able to hide you. The rocks will not cover you. You cannot be hidden from My presence when you try to hide sin in your life. You were bought with too high a price to allow you to move about in darkness.

I can pierce the darkest of souls and bring to light what needs to be confessed. Be forgiven and be thankful you still have Me to love you unconditionally. Experience My calling in a more clearer way than ever before.

You are Mine and I choose to reveal the love a father has for his child today. That is your need from Me and I fulfill it at this moment.

December 30

You are My child and will always have that relationship with you. You believe and yet you doubt sometimes at the same time. Even the fiercest warriors in My name had questions. They wanted to be sure what they were doing was for the right cause.

I had no problems with John the Baptist's doubts. He came face to face with the Savior and eventually was executed in My name. What is death after it has lost its sting? What is the grave after it was unable to extend its power over Me?

I will always love you. You have nothing to fear and don't worry about tomorrow. I AM already there.

December 31

As you wait on Me, I AM waiting on the right timing to move you to the next level of blessings. It will be waiting on you when you arrive. One won't have to wait, but will walk into My showers of blessings. It won't be a sprinkle. It will be more because of what you gave Me of your life.

You believed in Me when others doubted your beliefs about Me. You didn't fit in their theology box and saw you as a misfit. You didn't fit in because that was not the way I made you.

Don't look around and see how you can be like others. Look to Me for your identity and purpose. Make the best of every day and look for Me in ways you never looked before.

Read Ron P. Wallace's other book:

Encouraging Words
in a Discouraging World

Contact Ron
@
www.ronwallaceministries.com